THE SCHOOL IN QUESTION

*A Comparative Study of the School
and its Future in Western Society*

THE SCHOOL
IN QUESTION

*A Comparative Study of
the School and its Future
in Western Society*

TORSTEN HUSÉN

OXFORD UNIVERSITY PRESS
1979

Oxford University Press, Walton Street, Oxford OX2 6DP

OXFORD LONDON GLASGOW
NEW YORK TORONTO MELBOURNE WELLINGTON
KUALA LUMPUR SINGAPORE JAKARTA HONG KONG TOKYO
DELHI BOMBAY CALCUTTA MADRAS KARACHI
NAIROBI DAR ES SALAAM CAPE TOWN

Published in the United States by
Oxford University Press, New York

British Library Cataloguing in Publication Data

Husén, Torsten
The school in question.
1. Education – History – 20th century
I. Title
370'9181'2   LA132   79–40388

ISBN 0–19–874085–9
ISBN 0–19–874086–7 Pbk

Typesetting by Gloucester Typesetting Co Ltd
and printed in Great Britain by
Richard Clay (The Chaucer Press) Ltd,
Bungay, Suffolk

Contents

Foreword
by Alan Bullock

THE great merit of Professor Husén's book is in making a *comparative* study of the future of institutionalized schooling. Most of us when we discuss the problems of education talk about them in terms of one country, our own. Of course this is right insofar as the vertical, historical development of each society is unique and profoundly affects the character of the educational system. But Professor Husén's book brings out the importance of also looking at educational problems not only vertically, in an historical perspective, but at the same time horizontally, in a contemporary perspective.

Professor Husén's study is the product of a project organized by the Aspen Institute. Its origin goes back to a seminar held in Aspen, Colorado, for a fortnight in the summer of 1976 and devoted to the explosive question, What is an educated person in the last quarter of the 20th century? A record of this has been edited by Martin Kaplan. Stephen Graubard and I acted as co-chairmen and amongst those who took part were Lionel and Diana Trilling, Daniel Bell, Daniel Boorstin, William Bouwsma, Steve Weinberg, Carl Schorske, Martin Meyerson, Fred Dainton, Asa Briggs, Francis Keppel, Mortimer Adler and Eric Weil. A few months later a different group, this time involving Hellmut Becker, Max Kohnstamm, Torsten Husén, Jan Szcepanski and other Europeans took the same subject for discussion in the Aspen Institute, Berlin. There were a number of striking differences between the two, reflecting the very different ways in which a predominantly American and a predominantly European group approached the question. But the most important practical difference was our decision in Berlin to define a particular set of questions, amongst the variety of those thrown up, which would most repay further investigation.

We found the focus we were looking for in the future of secondary education and, even more important, found in

Torsten Husén a scholar with the rare, if not unique, qualifications required to look at the question in the context not of one
or two but of the whole group of advanced industrial countries
belonging to the OECD to which he has been educational
consultant for many years. He has also been able to draw upon
his experiences as a leader of the research team which conducted
an evaluation study of some twenty national systems of education. Thanks to this background he has had access to—has
indeed largely collected—data reflecting the experience of
countries as widely different in their historical development as
Canada and Japan, the U.S.A. and Sweden. It is on this basis,
and the personal acquaintance which he has acquired of
secondary education in such different contexts, that he has
framed a series of 'horizontal', across the board, general
propositions about the dissatisfaction with institutionalized
schooling at the secondary level which, he argues, is to be
found, in greater or less degree, in all of them.

I cannot believe there is anybody who has been involved in
thinking and arguing about education who will not find this
illuminating, for it powerfully suggests that many of the problems which we are inclined to think are specially characteristic
of our own society—whether that be England, the U.S.A.,
Germany or Japan—are to be found in others as well, and that
in turn suggests that they are not to be properly understood, or
remedied, if they are looked at in purely national (or, as so often,
in parochial) terms.

In making the inquiry a project in its continuing programme
on Education for a Changing Society, the Aspen Institute
undertook to secure the necessary funding (for which we are
indebted to the *Stifterverband für die Deutsche Wissenschaft*) and to
organize a number of workshops, both in Colorado and in
Berlin. At these Professor Husén was able to try out drafts
of his chapters and later, when the final draft was complete,
to discuss the implications of his analysis with a number
of those in a position to influence educational policy. The
comparative, international approach is characteristic of Aspen
programmes and we were fortunate in securing a core group of
participants closely associated with the work of the Institute
who took an active interest in the project throughout its life.
Amongst these should be mentioned Ernie Boyer, at the time

U.S. Commissioner for Education, and his predecessor in that office, Francis Keppel, now Director of the Institute's Education Programme; Hellmut Becker; Martin Meyerson; J. E. Slater, President of the Aspen Institute, and Shepard Stone, Director of the Aspen Institute, Berlin.

As a member of the group myself and a Trustee and Fellow of the Aspen Institute, I have been present at most of the meetings and I have been struck by the way in which the exchange between Professor Husén and the other participants worked to the advantage of both. There is no doubt that this is one man's book, not a committee report drafted by a rapporteur, or that it gains from the long personal experience of education and social research which has gone into it. Whenever we met, it was Torsten Husén's draft which provided the focus of our discussions; but no author was ever less concerned with defending his point of view or more open-minded in listening to and drawing from the contributions of others.

The purpose of this book, and of any other study sponsored by the Aspen Institute, is practical, to have an impact on policy making. Professor Husén himself, however, has steadily refused to conclude his study with a clear cut set of policy recommendations. The reason for this is not an insistence on academic neutrality but the experience of working, as he says in his final paragraph, with planners and policy makers at both national and international levels. This has taught him that it is not only useless but dangerous to draw up proposals which can all too easily become detached from the diagnosis of the situation and separated from each other into a 'shopping list' from which politicians can pick those that are most attractive in the short run.

Instead he has posed a set of questions which he argues should figure on the agenda of all who share in the responsibility of planning the future of education at the secondary level.

There is another obvious practical reason why this is a wise procedure. Although the questions arise out of a comparative study, of problems and discontents common to all the advanced industrial countries, the answers to his questions have got to be worked out in terms of each individual society with its own highly distinctive traditions, limitations and opportunities.

No one should underestimate the importance of finding

answers. We are in real danger throughout the industrialized world of building up a force of frustration in our young people which could disrupt our societies. Human beings between the age of puberty and, say, 25, are at their most creative and energetic; yet in all advanced societies there are steadily fewer opportunities for them to express their creativity and energy in the satisfaction of responsibility. What a comment on our societies, that in more than one Aspen seminar we have heard the phrase used: 'Youth is becoming redundant.' But young people will not submit to being treated as redundant, shut away from the real world in the institutions of secondary and higher education, frustrated when they come to look for jobs and denied an outlet for their energies. If we cannot provide a positive outlet for these energies, they will find expression—they already do, in many of our cities—in a destructive way.

The writing on the wall may be in the form of graffiti, but it is to be taken seriously. If we do not find better answers to the questions Torsten Husén has asked, we are likely to find the issues they raise amongst the most explosive on the political agenda of the future.

St. Catherine's College
University of Oxford
5 January 1979

ALAN BULLOCK

Author's Preface

THE 1960s was a decade of exponential growth of educational provision and school expenditures boosted by an almost euphoric belief in education. The 1970s has, under the influences of inflation and zero growth, witnessed a 'headlong retreat' from commitments to education. The school as an institution, particularly secondary school, has become the target of heavy criticism. Education has for some time been in a state of crisis of finance, confidence, and *raison d'être*.

Evidently, the 'crisis' (the appropriateness of the term was questioned at the Aspen–Berlin seminar in the autumn of 1976) reflected institutional shortcomings, both internal and external. The latter pertain to how formal education is related to other institutions and to society at large, not least to the world of work. A realization of these problems formed the starting-point of the Aspen Institute project on the future of schooling as an institution. In 1975 I was asked by Lord Alan Bullock, Aspen Trustee, and Dr. Francis Keppel, Director of the Aspen Educational Program, to prepare a memorandum on how I would conceive of such a project. In my view, the first step should be an attempt to identify cross-nationally the salient trends in present-day formal education, particularly at the secondary level, with the focus on the cardinal issues. A review of relevant literature, systematic fact-finding, and international seminar sessions and workshops were to be the instruments for clarifying issues and for discussing means of reshaping the school system in order to make it better fulfil its role in the society of today and tomorrow.

The project was launched in early 1976. A seminar was conducted in Aspen–Berlin later in the same year with participants from thirteen countries. The seminar identified and discussed 'crisis' symptoms, and attempts were made to account for them. Preliminary discussions were held about youth problems and reforms that were called for. A report from the seminar was published in the report series of the Aspen Institute, Berlin. The next step was to continue the literature review and to collate statistical and other evidence from the highly industrialized countries on certain important trends, for instance, demographic changes and their repercussions on enrolment and teacher demand. Additional studies dealt with cost development and youth unemployment.

Some of the statistical material was collected for a workshop on 'Education and Work' conducted at the Aspen Institute, Colorado, in July 1977. A working paper, 'Education and Work in the Policy Mix: International Comparisons', was prepared for the workshop which focused on youth problems as they evolved in the interplay between education and work. Youth unemployment and the 'fit' between education and work were the two concrete problem areas discussed by drawing upon data and experiences from the ten countries represented. The problems were, however, seen in the larger context of the status of youth in society today. The questions to what extent there is a 'youth problem' and whether there is any justification for talking about a 'generation gap' were dealt with at some length.

The second big international seminar took place at the Aspen Institute, Berlin, in September 1977, when the discussions focused on three major areas: (1) interaction between school and society, with particular reference to working life, the reward system, and its repercussions on the school; (2) decision-making and governance in school education in a system that tends to be caught between increased bureaucratization and vocal demands for participation on the part of teachers, parents, and students; (3) the 'inner life' of the school, both inside and outside the classroom, as determined by the structure and size of enrolment, work modes, examinations and tests, etc.

As part of a background to the project reported in the present book, an introductory biographical note would be in order. By training I am a psychologist but with a sociological slant I have devoted more than thirty years to studies of problems related to educational reform. Although I conducted my first studies in developmental and differential psychology, my interest in problems of educational reform made me broaden my perspective through the study of educational problems in their social and economic setting. Later I adopted cross-national, comparative views. My interest in how individual differences developed was, in the 1940s, conducive to studies of environmental influences on cognitive achievements and attempts to estimate the 'reserve of talent'. In 1948 a series of studies related to these problem areas were published in *Begåvning och miljö* (Ability and Environment). After many years when problems of educational reform and school structure had been the main preoccupation, the earlier line of inquiry was pursued in *Talent, Opportunity and Career* (1969) as well as in *Talent, Equality and Meritocracy* (1974b) and *Social Influences on Educational Attainment* (1975). A third line of inquiry, since 1960, has been international comparative surveys of student achievement as related to home background, school resources, and classroom practices (Husén, 1967).

The present project was conceived as a comprehensive attempt to identify the salient trends in European and American school education during the last few decades with particular emphasis on the 'crisis' in the late 1960s and early 1970s. What major problems are besetting school education? How do we account for them? What should be done with the youth school by way of reshaping the institution in order to come to grips with its problems?

The task that has been set is threefold: (1) to identify the 'crisis' symptoms, (2) to diagnose the 'disease' that accounts for the mismatch between school and society, and (3) to reassess the school as an institution. The ultimate purpose of the exercise is to arrive at a plausible scenario for the school of the future.

The overriding task is indeed an audacious, not to say an over-ambitious one. I dared to undertake it because I am convinced that a comprehensive look has to be taken at the school as an institution and at its present problems, in order to find out in what direction it is moving. By 'comprehensive' I mean that the perspective has to be widened far beyond the realms of classroom pedagogics to encompass how the educational system operates within its societal framework. The message that we get from the confused 'deschooling' debate is that the basic issues pertaining to the relationship between school and society need further clarification.

Apart from being the result of many years of educational research, particularly international comparative studies, what kind of credentials for the validity of the conclusions reached in this book can be claimed? The project has been conducted along three lines of inquiry. In the first place, the extensive literature published over the last decade on various 'crisis' symptoms and institutional problems has been reviewed; needless to say, without claims of complete or even representative coverage. Secondly, and assisted by Jeffrey Bulcock, I collected data and collated available national statistics relevant to some of the problem areas dealt with in this book. For instance, demographic and enrolment statistics from the OECD countries have been collated and their implications for teacher demand and cost development have been brought out. Thirdly, and most importantly, two international seminars have been conducted at the Aspen Institute, Berlin, and one international workshop on 'Education and Work' at the Aspen Institute, Aspen, Colorado. Prominent educators and scholars from fifteen countries have participated in discussing the issues on which the project has focused. The seminars have substantially contributed to the deepening of the analysis and to advancing proposals about how to come to grips with the problems that beset the school of today. The final manuscript has served as input to two workshops conducted respectively in Aspen, Colorado and in Berlin. In this connection I should also mention the interviews that I have conducted with colleagues around the world.

What is the 'ideological' basis of the present study? Over some twenty years I have been involved in policy-oriented research related to Swedish school reforms. In recent years I have been conducting international surveys focusing on policy problems of cross-national relevance. Since 1945 social scientists in many countries, not least in Sweden, have increasingly been called upon to put their competencies at the disposal of government commissions and agencies in studying social problems empirically. Studies of the quantitative, 'political–arithmetic' type gained momentum in the 1950s and early 1960s and were to provide policy makers and planners with an extended knowledge base for their decisions. This research on both sides of the Atlantic often took place in an atmosphere of undogmatic political radicalism of the liberal brand, which, to quote Karabel and Halsey (1977, p. 27), had 'its commitments . . . towards making a reality of the idea of the Welfare State'.

These circumstances should be mentioned because I cannot,

any more than other social scientists, claim ideological neutrality and detachment. The over-all ideology which permeates this book could be labelled social liberalism in the tradition indicated above of commitment to the Welfare State. The emphasis is on individual self-realization within the framework of the common good and on a social control exercised by the State that calls for the establishment of institutional checks aimed at preserving the common good. Highly industrialized societies, be they more planned and socialist or more market-oriented and capitalist, have increasingly established organs for the protection of the individual against the hazards of over-indulgence in economic self-promotion and for the prevention of repression and material poverty. An increased body of welfare legislation has resulted in a growing bureaucracy in charge of its implementation. The establishment of an extended financial basis for this has led to increased taxes.

By relieving the individual of the hazards of poverty, by providing more opportunities—not least by means of education—for self-development, and by limiting the arbitrary exercise of power by the holders of money and status, the margin of individual options has in certain respects been widened. The Social Democratic Party in Sweden, without putting too much emphasis on its socialist ideology, launched the slogan in election campaigns in the 1960s of a society with widened options.

Another point of liberal consensus is that one, if not the overriding, purpose of the educational system should be to help the individual to realize his potentialities, abilities, and interests as they develop from interaction amongst the various agents that constitute the 'ecology' of educative influences.

A cardinal issue in an achievement-oriented, highly industrial society is the right to meaningful employment, which is an issue of particular importance with a permanently high rate of youth unemployment. Young people are hit by a much higher rate of unemployment than adults. The problem seems relatively independent of business cycles. In spite of being equipped with more formal education than previous generations, young people in the highly industrialized countries meet increased difficulties in entering the labour market.

The studies presented in this book sweep over wide waters, and can be seen as an attempt on my part to structure the experiences gained during a long career as an educational researcher and reformer. In order to keep the length of the book within reasonable limits, it has been quite impossible to provide all the statistical and other evidence necessary to document the statements to the extent customary in specialized scholarly reports. Nor has it been possible to list all the references which have served as background material. At the end of the book I have listed the major works to which reference has been made. The original research that was part of the project, for instance enrolment changes and cost development, will be reported in full detail elsewhere by Jeffrey Bulcock. Here I have presented it in summary form only.

I have not entertained an ambition to come up with concrete, clear-cut 'solutions', not to mention panaceas, to the problems that beset the school. I have, however, been ambitious enough to try to identify major issues and describe their nature. Such endeavours are more proper for social scientists than advancing lists of 'recommendations'. The attempt to pin-point the issues also means an attempt to put the school problems of today into perspective.

Even though I have drafted the manuscript of the present book and, of course, have to take responsibility for its short-comings, I cannot alone take credit for whatever might be considered its merits. Not least the seminar sessions provided me with a valuable input of experiences and wisdom from out-standing educators and scholars. Participants in the seminars sponsored by the Aspen Institute for Humanistic Studies both in Berlin and Aspen, Colorado, have been listed on page 182.

I want to thank Dr. Jeffrey Bulcock of the Memorial University of Newfoundland who readily accepted to spend a year with me as a Research Associate. Dr. Bulcock was in charge of the research that dealt with statistical trends, such as demographic changes and cost development. Furthermore, he prepared the reports from the international seminars, from which I have also been able to draw in the writing of this book.

Sponsoring bodies have in various ways supported and facilitated the venture which is reported here. I already mentioned that Lord Alan Bullock and Dr. Francis Keppel in various capacities facilitated and supported the study. Dr. Joseph Slater, President of the Aspen Institute for Humanistic

Studies, Colorado, and Dr. Shepard Stone of the Aspen Institute, Berlin, have stimulated the study with their keen interest and support. The international seminars and workshops in Berlin and Aspen respectively have been instrumental in giving the study a proper perspective. The *Stifterverband für die Deutsche Wissenschaft* covered a major portion of the costs incurred by a generous grant.

I am also deeply indebted to those who have generously taken time and trouble to subject the first draft of the manuscript to critical reading which it badly needed, not least since English is my third language. Jeffrey Bulcock, Alan Bullock, Michael Haltzel, Francis Keppel, and Harry Passow have gone through the manuscript partly or in its entirety.

My secretary, Mrs. Birgitta Horn, has skilfully helped me with the documentation and the preparation of the manuscript.

Stockholm, 1978 TORSTEN HUSÉN

I

Introduction: The 'Crisis' and
its Symptoms

FROM EUPHORIA TO DISENCHANTMENT

THE nineteenth century saw universal elementary schooling emerge in the Western world. By the First World War it was fully implemented in the industrial nations. The Second World War marked another upsurge of formal education. Secondary schooling at the junior level began after 1945 to become universal. By the late 1960s, universal tertiary education began to be seriously contemplated within the framework of a 'lifelong', 'recurrent', or 'permanent' system of education.

But at the very peak of its dazzling success, in the almost euphoric moment of being conceived as the prime instrument of individual self-realization, social progress, and economic prosperity, education began to be beset by doubts about what schools were achieving and serious criticisms were launched. The school as an institution came under severe attack and in some quarters there was talk about a 'crisis', even a world-wide one. At the 1967 Williamsburg meeting of some 150 leading educators from all over the world, organized on the initiative of President Johnson, the theme for the deliberations was 'world crisis in education', which was also the title of the main working paper (Coombs, 1968). It is indeed worthwhile to look at the education scene of 1967 in retrospect.

At that time, the scope of the 'crisis' was not fully grasped. The main concern was the discrepancy between demand and supply of education, in terms both of available facilities, such as school buildings, teachers, and teaching material, and of financial means. The papers and recommendations were typically published under the subtitle *The Crisis of Supply and Demand*

(Bereday, 1969). Even if other inadequacies, such as lack of curricular relevance, were mentioned, the analysis did not bring into question the institution as such. No mention was made of student reactions and the quest for participation or of alternative institutional arrangements, such as free schools. Yet there were already in 1967 signs of an incipient student revolt in Germany.

Few people took a critical look at available demographic information which would have made them consider implications for enrolment in higher education. The preoccupation with the problems of the day seemed to loom so large that even planners who were supposed to take long-range views were blind to the signs that could be read on the walls. The lack of foresight in the 1960s could otherwise not be explained. The effects of the baby-boom were seldom projected into the educational system, and economic projections did not take into account the possibility of recessions.

What nobody predicted in the early 1960s has actually happened; namely the value of the school as an institution has been brought into question, and to such an extent that quite a few people have taken the 'deschooling' movement spearheaded by Illich (1970) seriously.

The crisis is now viewed as symptomatic of institutional shortcomings, both internal ones and those that pertain to the relationships between formal education and other institutions in society, not least the world of work. Misgivings are particularly strong about secondary education and are reflected in the large number of commissions and task forces, public and private, which have been inquiring in recent years in both Europe and North America into the role of secondary schooling not only in its relation to other stages in the educational system but also in its relations to working life. The transition from education to work and the youth unemployment problem have, over the last few years, become focal points in the debate and in the various inquiries into how adequate the educational system is in present-day society. The signs of a loss of confidence mainly relate to formal school education, whereas adult education and out-of-school education in general have gained higher priority.

By the mid-1970s a sombre mood had replaced the strong commitment to education of the mid-1960s. Euphoria gave way to disenchantment.

'CRISIS' SYMPTOMS

1. Education and Politics

The most evident symptom of changed attitudes towards education is the wave of criticism from both left and right that swept
many countries in the late 1960s. The former consensus about
the benefits of traditional schooling and the conviction that
education always represented an intrinsic good were gone. So
was the belief that education was the main instrument for
bringing about a better society. The conservatives blamed the
school for its low academic standards, its lack of discipline, and
for neglecting the talented students. The radical left accused
the schools of being joyless, oppressive, and autocratic. A new
breed of Marxist educators perceived schools as instruments of
capitalist society. Schools were there to produce a work-force
that would fit the hierarchical and oppressive working life in
that type of society.

A by-product of the debate was the growing awareness that
the schools of a given country operate within a given social and
economic framework, whereas prior to the 1960s school problems were often conceived of as purely pedagogical ones that
emerged in a socio-economic vacuum. This widening of the
perspective has been beneficial to the debate, because it has led
to the realization that problems besetting the educational system
are in the last analysis social problems which cannot be solved
simply by taking action only within the walls of the school. Such
a view has consistently been supported by large-scale surveys,
for instance the Coleman (1966) study on equality of educational opportunity in the United States, and the Plowden survey
of 11-year-olds in England (HMSO, 1967), as well as the
twenty-country comparative evaluation study conducted by the
International Association for the Evaluation of Educational
Achievement (IEA) (Husén, ed., 1967 and Walker, 1976). These
studies consistently show that social background and home conditions account for a larger portion of the between-student and
the between-school differences in cognitive outcomes than do
school resources and teaching practices.

2. Commissions of Inquiry

The school covering the age range 14 to 18 has been a favourite

target of criticism. Most of the work devoted by various commissions to school reforms on both sides of the Atlantic has gone
into attempts to come to grips with problems in secondary
education. Irrespective of confounding social problems, the
mere fact that in Europe from the early 1950s to 1970s a rapid
change took place whereby the elitist character of secondary
education was transformed into an institution of mass, or even
universal, membership has put the secondary school under
heavy adaptive strains which take a long time to overcome.

The response to the 'tumultuous' 1960s has typically been to
create commissions to study the problems of youth. In the
United States five commissions have since the early 1970s
inquired into the secondary school crisis and advanced recommendations for improving the situation. The most important of
these is the Panel on Youth of the President's Science Advisory
Committee that in 1974 submitted its report *Youth: Transition to
Adulthood* (Coleman *et al.*, 1974). It was chaired by the Chicago
sociologist James S. Coleman, who earlier had conducted path-
breaking studies of what he called the 'adolescent society'
(Coleman, 1961). The report by the Panel on Youth has had a
strong and fruitful impact on the debate about fundamental
youth and school problems in industrial society.

3. *Education and Equality*

The change in mood and aspirations can be assessed by comparing the reports from two major OECD conferences on educational policy and its implications for economic growth, the
first one in Washington, D.C. in 1961 (OECD, 1962) and the
second in Paris in 1970 (OECD, 1971b). At the 1961 conference education was depicted as the major instrument of
social welfare and change, and as a booster of economic growth.
In the same year OECD sponsored a seminar in Kungälv,
Sweden, on equality of educational opportunity (Halsey, 1961)
where equal and rational utilization of ability from all social
strata was considered to be a powerful way of promoting welfare and economic growth. The 1971 report is less optimistic.
The rapporteurs point out that the goals set for educational
policy a decade earlier had not been achieved. For example,
expansion of educational facilities and increased enrolment had

not contributed to the equalization of educational opportunities to the extent expected. The disparities among social strata in participation prevailed by moving up the educational ladder.

Formal education was seen by nineteenth-century liberals as an instrument of equalization which in Horace Mann's words would be 'a great equalizer of the conditions of men, the balance-wheel of the social machinery . . . It does better than disarm the poor of their hostility toward the rich: It prevents being poor . . .' (quoted after Schrag, 1970). Education was further regarded as a prime instrument for the individual born under humble circumstances to move up the social ladder. Everybody was to be given equal opportunity to achieve, provided he had the talent and energy. Those who failed under such circumstances were considered either stupid, or lazy, or both. In our achievement-oriented society it has become increasingly evident that 'some are more equal than others' and that formal equality does not guarantee equality of life chances even in socialist societies strongly committed to equalization.

4. *Negativism in the Classroom*

There is ample evidence to show that in highly industrialized countries, such as the United States, the Netherlands, or the Federal Republic of Germany, attitude towards school becomes increasingly negative as the students progress through the grades constituting compulsory schooling. Even among those who opt to proceed through the upper secondary school the general attitude tends towards the negative side. Representative samples of 10-year-olds, 14-year-olds, and students in the last grade of the pre-university school were surveyed by the International Association for the Evaluation of Educational Achievement (IEA). On the basis of an inventory of statements, such as 'I should like to have as much education as I can possibly get', a 'Like School' scale was constructed (Husén *et al.*, 1973).

A consistent deterioration of attitudes over all the countries from the 10- to the 14-year-old level was found. In countries where 15- or 16-year-olds were investigated as a national option, comparisons could be made over the last three grades of compulsory school. Low-performing students and students with underprivileged home backgrounds tended to show the most marked, progressively negative, attitudes.

The most pronounced negativism was found in affluent, industrialized countries, whereas students in developing countries with miserable school resources showed a much more positive attitude towards schooling. Lacking further analyses of these data, the best explanation that can be advanced is simply that in affluent countries there are many agents that compete in attracting the attention of young people, such as the mass media, various leisure-time activities, and sports.

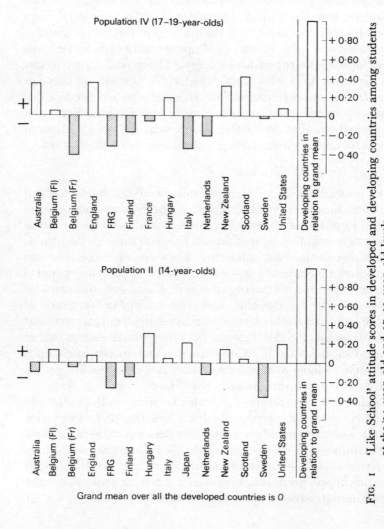

Fig. 1 'Like School' attitude scores in developed and developing countries among students at the 14-year-old and 17–19-year-old levels.

Source: Husén *et al.* (1973, p. 162).

5. *The Diminishing Priority of Education*

There are clear indications that educational policy has slipped down the political priority scale. For instance, in 1970 the Brandt Government in the Federal Republic of Germany presented an elaborate document on educational policy (*Bildungsbericht*, 1970). Certain basic problems related to the reform of German education were regarded as top policy issues in the election campaign. A few years later opinion polls gave clear indications that educational policy no longer captured the attention of the electorate to the same degree. This is *one* reason why the policy outlined in the *Bildungsbericht* has to a large extent not been implemented.

A summing up of what has—and has not—happened with German school reform, and the reasons why, were discussed in a series of articles in *Die Zeit* that later appeared in book form (Becker *et al.*, 1976). Hellmut Becker begins his first article on the shortcomings of German educational policy by stating: 'Education is at present not "in". Both right and left agree on this. The far left thinks that the school reform in the first place was never really intended, in the second place has not occurred and, if it ever occurred, would have been an instrument of reinforcing the power of the ruling class.' The conception of the problems besetting the German school is characterized by a striking polarization. 'The arguments are contradictory but the dissatisfaction is shared.' (p. 9) For instance, on the one hand the school is accused of being too demanding and of exerting a 'terror of marks'. On the other hand, there are vociferous allegations that the school is too sloppy and not demanding enough.

The diagnosis that Becker ventures for the German situation has applicability also in other countries where things did not work out according to the intentions of the reformers. He points out that the profound changes implied in a school reform require *simultaneous* changes of structures and content over the entire system from kindergarten to university. A prerequisite for such a change to be implemented is a change in the whole set of attitudes that determine how teachers, parents, and others concerned conceive the functions of the school. 'The release of education from its established order, from its taboos, and from its traditional canons is bound to produce quite a lot of uncertainty.' (p. 12) The state of flux has, of course, fostered the political polarization that has had repercussions on issues which used to be far from the political battlefield, such as the teaching of the 'new maths'.

Fred Hechinger (1976) has reviewed the change that has occurred on the American scene under the provocative title 'Murder in Academe: The Demise of Education'. He points out that what makes the present situation in the U.S. so serious is the fact that education is under attack from two opposite directions: 'In the past, when education had to ward off only the attacks from the reactionary right, the consequences were confined to occasional short-term setbacks. The expansive forward thrust was never deflected for long. Popular faith in each generation's capacity to do better than its predecessor was inseparably linked to education as, in Horace Mann's words, the "great equalizer" and society's "balance-wheel". ' (p. 11)

6. *Budgetary cuts*

The most tangible sign of loss of confidence is budgetary cuts. There is talk about a 'management of decline' in school education. In the late 1950s and early 1960s increased demand for education reflected in exponentially expanding enrolments was met within the existing institutional framework. The provision of more formal education for an increased length of time was seldom questioned. Heavily augmented public expenditures on education in the highly industrialized countries of Western Europe and North America were backed not only by the human capital theory but also by a solid consensus about the benefits of education accruing to both the individual and society. Thus, these expenditures were allowed to increase their share of the GNP from 2–3 per cent in the 1950s to 6–8 per cent in the late 1960s. The unit cost, that is to say, the cost per student and year in constant prices, doubled in several countries during the 1960s.

The operating costs in education have now reached a critical level. As long as the economy grew by some 5 per cent a year and as long as education was treated almost as a sacred cow, a cost increase of 15 per cent a year did not give rise to serious concern. With reduced growth or even zero growth, a labour-intensive industry such as education by necessity becomes subject to tough priorities that have to be established not only among education and other domains in the public sector but among levels in education as well. The repercussions of a non-growth situation tend to be particularly strong on formal schooling, especially at the post-compulsory level, where the cost increases have been very steep.

7. Institutionalization and its Consequences

Alarming reports of the state of affairs in the classroom have been forthcoming since the end of the 1960s. The most famous of these reports is Charles Silberman's *Crisis in the Classroom*, published in 1970 after three-and-a-half years of inquiry and visits to many schools all over the United States. Within the framework of a broad perspective on the social role of the school, Silberman presents a long series of illustrative examples from everyday life in school.

A key problem in educating teenagers in our society is to promote what I have labelled 'functional participation'. Only a few decades ago young people, particularly in Europe, were absorbed early into the adult world. They had to learn by the early teens to assume responsibility, since they had to begin to support themselves after six or seven years in elementary school. Even before that they had experienced working with adults at home. Now they tend to be kept separate, simply because the adult world and the youth world are kept separate by the institutional arrangements. In today's urbanized society young people often have very vague notions of what their parents are kept busy with. Few of them are drawn into adult affairs and given an opportunity to shoulder adult responsibilities.

These general observations also apply to the school. The reality outside the school, the world for which the school allegedly prepares young people, is mediated by the printed and spoken word. The transition from the 'information-rich but action-poor' school to working life is often a traumatic experience. Young people coming directly from school are not ready to shoulder adult responsibilities after their many years of schooling. Starting at the age of 5 to 7 and proceeding to at least the age of 15 or 16 (the majority is now in several countries staying in school until the age of 17 or 18), the students have become used to having their work planned in detail by the teachers hour after hour, day after day, year after year. The subject matter set out in syllabuses has been carefully prepared and dutifully parcelled out by the educators, whose worst nightmare is that the clock will run out on them before they finish the course. The result of such extended institutionalization has been serious problems of motivation and discipline, which two educational psychologists, DeCecco and Richards (1975), refer to as 'civil war in the high schools'. Moreover the benefits in terms of increased competence during the last few years of compulsory schooling are in many cases, as shown by the IEA survey, only marginal. A staggering number of students are functional illiterates after 8–10 years of formal schooling (HMSO, 1975).

In sum, there are three major reasons why schools, and in particular universities, became in the 1960s arenas of social and political conflict. (1) As already pointed out, expenditures on education had grown rapidly, twice as fast as the GNP and one-and-a-half to two times the rate of total public expenditure. This gave rise to demands for accountability, for basic reappraisal and reform of the entire system, and for public control with all that this implies in political controversy. (2) Education was increasingly perceived of as, and to some extent became, an instrument for enhanced life chances and career promotion. As enrolment soared the competition for marks and access to higher education rapidly became tougher. The ideology of equality of educational opportunity boosted the aspirations among parents and their offspring in social strata which previously had not had access to advanced education. These aspirations were partly thwarted in a situation of heightened competition where those of culturally privileged home background tended to be more successful. Many who made it all the way through higher education discovered by the early 1970s that they were 'over-educated' for the job market. (3) The traditional bureaucratic and hierarchical administration and governance of the educational system came into conflict with demands for student and parent participation.

Thus we have, over a short time, moved quite a distance from where we were in the early 1960s, when education was still regarded as the panacea for social problems and ills. It was expected to cure us of poverty and to achieve greater equality of life chances. Education was almost entirely identified with formal schooling which benefited both the individual and society. Manpower planners were euphoric about investment in education. The euphoria of the 1960s was strong enough to allow expenditures on education to grow exponentially.

'CRISIS'—RHETORIC OR REALITY?

In view of experiences gained during the last decade we do not need further evidence to support the assertion that the school as an institution is in trouble—some say in deep trouble. To talk about 'crisis' is perhaps to overdramatize, but it is significant that the term has frequently appeared in book titles and speeches by leading public figures on issues in education. At the Aspen–Berlin seminar in 1976 some participants took exception to the use of the term which they regarded as rhetoric that tended to obscure the concrete problems. This is one reason why 'crisis' has been put within quotation marks.

Considering the discrepancy between the grand objectives depicted in school rhetoric on the one hand and the realities of the classroom on the other, it is sometimes too easy to resort to the term 'crisis' in describing how hopes and expectations shatter against harsh constraints, be they financial, administrative, or pedagogical. The term 'crisis' would seem more appropriate in characterizing the relationship between school and society than in describing the problems within the school. Most contemporary problems in formal schooling, for instance financial ones, have their counterparts in problems besetting other institutions in society. 'Crises' in society at large have repercussions on the school system. The neo-Marxist would in the short-term perspective interpret the present 'crisis' as an outcome of temporary 'structural contradictions' affecting the division of labour, to which the school as an institution would have to adapt. In the long term, industrial societies may be viewed as being in a state of flux between one paradigm, the industrial, and the next, the post-industrial.

Criticisms of the School as an Institution

UNIVERSAL elementary schooling in the nineteenth century was essential in establishing the infrastructure of the modern industrial nation-state in the Western world. After the Second World War schooling was extended to make junior and then senior secondary education universal. Universal tertiary education within a 'recurrent' framework began seriously to be contemplated in the early 1970s (OECD, 1973). Then criticisms began to be voiced more and more frequently.

I shall in this Chapter briefly review the criticisms levelled and the issues raised by radical and conservative critics. The politically radical critics have been of two kinds: the 'neo-Rousseauians' with an anarchistic leaning, such as Ivan Illich (1970) and Paul Goodman (1962), and the neo-Marxists, such as Samuel Bowles (1971), Martin Carnoy (1974), Henry Levin (1977), and Bowles and Herbert Gintis (1976). The neo-Rousseauians want to 'deschool' society entirely, whereas the neo-Marxists want to preserve the school as an institution but to reshape it so as to serve and match a society with a new order of production.

The conservative critics contend that standards, particularly basic skills, have continuously been slipping. They further argue that schools should be differentiated and thus be made more responsive to the 'natural' differences in abilities and bents among students.

CONSERVATIVE CRITICISM

Conservative criticism of the school during the last few decades has consisted of four main accusations:

(1) The broadening of access to institutions at the secondary and post-secondary levels has lowered the standards.

(2) Intellectual rigour and work discipline have deteriorated because of the removal of incentives, such as marks and competitive examinations, and because of more emphasis on affective objectives and social development than on cognitive achievements.

(3) Gifted children have been neglected as a consequence of the acceptance of dogmatic egalitarianism according to which there are no inherent human differences, and therefore no reason to differentiate between more and less able pupils.

(4) Labour-market-oriented education has yielded to an equality-oriented one which overemphasizes the custodial functions of the school.

The titles of two of the most discussed books, *Educational Wastelands* by Arthur Bestor (1953) and *Quackery in the Public Schools* by Albert Lynd (1953), are illuminating. Both Bestor and Lynd collected considerable evidence of lack of intellectual rigour and the deterioration of basic skills. The debate was further exacerbated by the Sputnik psychosis in the late 1950s when the Soviet advantage in satellite technology was attributed in some quarters to more efficient teaching, particularly in science and mathematics, in Soviet secondary and higher education.

Most critics of mass secondary education on both sides of the Atlantic were speaking on behalf of the universities, which were the main recipients of the products of secondary schools. The criticisms in the United States in the early 1950s reflected a process of rapid change combined with spectacular expansion of the high school. The universalization of secondary schooling led to the establishment of a highly differentiated system of programmes and courses that could cater for all young people of secondary school age. But the notion of the academically-oriented high school still prevailed among university teachers who found that the secondary school fell shockingly short of expected standards. Their disappointment added a considerable amount of fuel to the fire set by Sputnik. European countries had similar experiences after the period of rapid expansion of secondary school enrolment.

A favourite target of the criticism was progressive education or 'life adjustment education'. We cannot know, the argument ran, whether the society the child will be confronted with as an adult will be the same as the one in which he is growing up. Conditions change rapidly. The nuclear age poses problems different from those of an earlier society. We can be confident, however, that the historic reality with which we are confronted in literature, history, philosophy, and languages is the source of our own culture and will provide the perspective necessary to increase our understanding of present society and our own role in it.

Progressive education during the early 1950s in the United States—the McCarthy period—was in certain circles regarded as being communistic and subversive. I remember a conversation in 1954 with the Dean of one of the more prominent schools of education who told me that courses in the philosophy of education had come under political attack because they were accused of spreading 'subversive' ideas.

The principles upon which progressive education was built were essentially these. Education should be 'child-centered', that is to say, based on the child's 'real' needs. The content of education, the school curriculum, should reflect 'life adjustment' by providing knowledge and skills that would prove useful in the child's later life. Education should match the level of development of the child.

Many of the attacks against progressivism were levelled at John Dewey, whose philosophy was supposed to have been behind the progressive 'movement' which in several instances was also identified with political radicalism. Consider Counts's (1932) reconstructivism, which regarded education as an instrument of bringing about radical social reforms. But Dewey himself was the first to point out that underlying the excesses of progressivism at the classroom level was a confusion between goals and means in his educational philosophy. Child-centred education was not a goal but a means of achieving better results, more efficient education.

Conant's (1959a) investigation of the American comprehensive high school helped to restore the balance in the debate and put the issues in a proper perspective. In studying a sample of high schools he applied three criteria. (1) To what extent did the school provide a good general education for all students? (2) To what extent did the school provide at least those students who did not go on to post-secondary education with marketable skills? (3) To what extent was the school catering for the academically gifted students? Very few of the comprehensive schools visited by Conant and his team lived up to all three criteria. The recommendations of the main report underlined the necessity of limiting the cafeteria system of options and providing a core curriculum of general subjects for all students, with enough margin for options to fit individual differences in interest and abilities. Conant further recommended that the more able students be provided with the opportunity and given encouragement to take the more demanding academic courses, not least in mathematics and science—those areas of special concern during the Sputnik psychosis.

In a sequel to his main report, Conant (1959b) pointed out that the college professors who had criticized the comprehensive high school conceived of it as if it operated in a social vacuum. It is, he said, convenient to stick to the fiction that in the morning all the children come to school with the same intellectual gifts, interests, and motivation and that they return in the afternoon to homes which are all equally stimulating and interested in how the children get along in school. Moreover, it is also convenient for the critics of the school to maintain that the surrounding society has no other interest in the school than to assign to it the task of developing the intellectual capabilities of the children. But this is, indeed, wishful thinking that ignores the social framework of the school, which has to serve children from a rich variety of backgrounds, children from *all* families, not only 'my children and the children of my friends'.

HUMANISTIC CRITICISM: ROBERT M. HUTCHINS

During the Cold War with its pressures for conformity, the late Robert Hutchins (1953), in a series of lectures given at the University of Uppsala, Sweden, spelled out a philosophy of education that represented a counterview to the then prevailing pragmatic and positivistic emphasis. His criticism of the mainstream philosophy as represented, for instance, by the Educational Policies Commission in the United States, focused on three doctrines which by that time were held as self-evident truths by many American educators.

The first doctrine was that of adaptation or 'life adjustment education', whose object was 'to fit the student into his physical, social, political, economic, and intellectual environment with a minimum of discomfort to the society' (p. 13). The misconceived pragmatism with a strong emphasis on vocational training or career education is, according to Hutchins, 'poor mechanics without education'. The doctrine of adjustment to the 'demands' of the environment easily leads to a curriculum of disconnected and dead facts. Worst of all, life adjustment education overlooks that 'our mission here on earth is to change our environment, not to adjust ourselves to it'. (p. 16) The objective of adjustment easily leads to indoctrination and is opposed to the true spirit of democracy at the heart of which is criticism.

The second doctrine was that of education as the satisfaction of immediate or *ad hoc* needs, which reflected the view that what was of direct and immediate value to the individual as a citizen and as a bread-winner should be particularly emphasized in curriculum planning and classroom instruction. Skills in repairing household articles were seen as being more important than Latin, driver education as more important than history, and so on. The main limitation of such a doctrine is its inapplicability to a society of rapid change. Current information and current needs do not stay current for long. The specific pieces of knowledge required are too many and too diverse, so that implementation of such a philosophy leads to a disintegration of the school curriculum, which at the secondary and the university levels adopts a cafeteria-like character. It leads to the fragmentation of knowledge and a degree of specialization that destroys generalists and the unity of learning.

The third doctrine was that of no doctrine at all. Before the Second World War the reconstructionalists forcefully maintained that the school should serve as an instrument for social change. But how can one work for change once the goals have been achieved? More important, one has to know what values should guide the improvements in order to achieve these goals. The prevailing pragmatist or positivist philosophy provides no value guidelines. The basis for all thought and action in education should according to this view be scientific knowledge, not a set of values. But in order to improve mankind one has to have an idea what improvement is. Thus one has to have a 'true' doctrine. 'If the object of education is the improvement of men, then any system of education that is without values is a contradiction in terms.' (p. 48)

The malaise, then, that in the pragmatic age besets education is the lack of realization of the supremacy of values. A true education must include a study of values, and this cannot be done in a system designed to train specialists. The restoration of learning means the restoration of liberal education for the improvement of man. 'The object of liberal education in youth is not to teach the young all they will ever need to know. It is to give them the habits, ideas, and techniques that they need to continue to educate themselves.' (p. 49)

NEO-ROUSSEAUIAN 'DESCHOOLERS'

The 'new' criticism that emerged in the late 1960s was more fundamental: it was directed against the school as an institution. Most prominent among these critics were Ivan Illich (1970), Everett Reimer (1971), and Niels Christie (1971), whose book *Hvis skolen ikke fantes* (If the School Did Not Exist) represents a more constructive approach to the deschooling problem than the more doctrinaire one presented by Illich in *Deschooling Society*. Illich's critique was threefold:

(1) The school in both capitalist and socialist societies is an oppressive and monopolistic instrument.

(2) The school in today's specialized and consumer-oriented society serves to manipulate people.

(3) The school, particularly in the Third World, is serving only the élite in the modern sector and is degrading those who are in the traditional sector; it is reinforcing the meritocratic element in society by participating in a repressive ritual of upward social mobility. The masses are lured into believing that education is a status-providing and liberating instrument, whereas it simply serves to make them addictively dependent on the services of a formal system of education.

In an anthology that discusses his deschooling philosophy Illich says: 'School is the initiation to a society oriented toward the progressive consumption of increasingly less tangible and more expensive services, a society that relies on worldwide

standards, large-scale and long-term planning, constant obso-
lescence through the built-in ethos of never-ending improvements: the constant translation of new needs into specific
demands for the consumption of new satisfactions.' (Gartner
et al., 1973)

Illich places the formal educational system in a larger social
and economic context constituted by the modern bureaucratized 'service' society with its blurring of the borderline between
treatment and care. The latter has become increasingly institutionalized and has come under the control of technocrats. The
school, in fact, is paradigmatic of the development of the service
society. It is a monopolistic instrument of the consumer society
designed to manipulate people as early as possible in their life
and to prepare them for the roles of docile workers and consumers. The school is part of the monolithic welfare bureaucracy
which conveys the message that no learning is possible without
schooling; that the school knows both what is 'right' and how
to instil competencies. To cure or teach oneself is not only pre-
tentiously inappropriate, it is almost subversive.

The consequences of this system, therefore, have been counter
to the rhetoric of equality and self-realization. The school cannot achieve the alleged equality of life chances simply because
schooling and certification, as well as education and social role
occupancy, are closely connected. The 'diploma disease' (Dore,
1976) or credentialism (Berg, 1971) is a reflection of the manipulation of the educational system by market forces. Instead of
being an equalizer, the school creates class differences; it
polarizes society.

The school is unsuitable as a provider of either skills or
genuine education because it does not differentiate between
these two tasks. The training of skills and competencies for
specific jobs occurs according to a certain timetable, a curriculum in a literal sense, with a preset sequence of learning
events. True education is an interactive process between a
teacher and a student with a wide margin of indeterminism or
unpredictability. It is furthermore an activity in partnership
which is allergic to the mandatory atmosphere prevailing in the
school mill. Everything is predetermined and in the last analysis
steered by a huge bureaucracy. This runs counter to true education—a theme I shall address below in Chapter 7.

As Reimer (1971) puts it: the school is an institution that promises unlimited success to an unlimited number of people. This is particularly striking if one observes what is happening in the developing countries, where over the last few decades formal schooling of the European type has been introduced. Enrolments have been soaring. There is at all stages a tremendous drive for more and more years of school education. No stage has a profile of its own but is merely a preparation for the next stage. Since the important thing is the credential, the content of schooling is neglected. In a country like Botswana with a subsistence economy and a very small modern sector, some 60 per cent of the primary school leavers expect to go on to senior secondary education or beyond, in spite of the fact that a maximum of only 20 per cent could be accommodated in junior secondary school (Husén, 1977b). The majority of students expect to enter the modern sector in spite of the fact that for the foreseeable future cattle raising and crop farming will constitute the backbone of the country's economy.

NEO-MARXIST CRITICISM AND REASSESSMENT OF THE HISTORY OF COMPULSORY SCHOOLING

The neo-Marxists (e.g., Gintis, 1973), although agreeing with the description of the crisis symptoms, disagree with Illich about the diagnosis. They think that his analysis is too simplistic. One cannot stop at an analysis of the school in terms of manipulation of consumer behaviour; rather, one has to go deeper into the dynamics of the modern economic system. In order to understand what is really happening one has to study the productive forces and the inter-group relationships of working life. The school through its methods and internal relationships is preparing young people for the relations that prevail in the working life of modern society and the alienation that occurs as a consequence.

Therefore, Gintis argues, a quest for 'deschooling' is futile. The alienation can be overcome only by participatory and decentralized control in all sectors of society, in the factory, in the community, and in the school. A 'radical theory of educational reform becomes viable only by envisioning liberating and equal education as serving and becoming served by a radically altered nexus of social relations in *production*' (Gintis, 1973, p.31)

The most comprehensive attempt to advance a Marxist interpretation of how public schools in the capitalist world are established and operate is the one by Bowles and Gintis (1976). The formal system of schooling, according to the correspondence principle, is set up in order to reproduce the existing social and economic order. The schools are organized in the same way as modern corporations with the purpose of 'educating' young people to become disciplined and docile workers. The schools, then, exist to prepare young people for their future roles in the capitalist economy. They are sorting and sifting institutions which distribute status. The 'technocratic–meritocratic' ideology of equal educational opportunity serves as a kind of opium for the people.

Carnoy (1974) makes another attempt using radical social philosophy to formulate a comprehensive theory of how schooling is related to society. Basically the school as an institution is seen as a link between the economic and social structure of society on one hand, and the minds of children on the other. The common, public school is a product of the capitalist era. It helped to transform society from feudalism to capitalism. 'Like any other social organization, capitalism produced institutions that supported capitalist structures. So schools functioned to control social change (to maintain order), to produce better labor inputs for more material output, and to transform individuals into competitive men and women who functioned well and believed in the capitalist system.' (p. 5) Once society has entered the capitalist stage the school is there to prepare individuals to assume their various roles in the existing social and economic order.

It has long been assumed that by raising the average level of education one would bring about greater equality of status and life chances. Throughout the nineteenth century progressive industrialists and liberals thought that schooling liberated people by making them more competent and more prepared to participate in life on a more equal footing. But existing evidence does not give much support to this assumption. Differences in wealth and income seem to remain unchanged or only slightly reduced in a society with a high average level of formal education. Furthermore, even though education in the period of transformation from a traditional to a modern industrial society seems to assist people in escaping from traditional hierarchies, it creates new hierarchies and dependencies. It is a process that causes alienation.

Some radical critics of today's system of formal schooling have taken a complete reassessment of the history of popular, universal education as their point of departure. Michael Katz (1968) is an advocate of such a reappraisal: 'Americans share a warm and comforting myth about the origins of popular education. For the most part historians have helped to perpetuate this essentially noble story, which portrays a rational, enlightened working class, led by idealistic and humanitarian intellectuals, triumphantly wresting free public education from a selfish, wealthy elite and from the bigoted proponents of orthodox religion.' (p. 1) Katz challenges this myth by asking questions about what would seem to be unresolvable discrepancies between myth and reality. How could purely humanitarian attempts to bring education to the masses, particularly in big cities, result in the establishment of rigid bureaucracy and drill? Were educational reforms and innovations primarily products of the aspirations of the working class or of other class interests?

Katz tries to get answers to these and related questions by examining the development of public education in mid-nineteenth century Massachusetts, when industrialization, urbanization, and immigration all accelerated. The answer to the questions posed is that 'reform efforts have been spear-headed by the socially and intellectually prominent concerned for the preservation of domestic tranquillity and an ordered, cohesive society'. (p. 213) This élite 'group has been joined and supported by middle-class parents anxious about the status of their children and, somewhat tardily, for the most part, by the organized schoolmen, who understandably enough have evaluated reform theory in terms of its impact upon their own precarious status'. (pp. 213–14)

The most vocal supporters of educational reform were those whose talent and money 'helped usher in an industrial society. Deeply ambivalent toward the society for which they were responsible, social leaders sought innovations that would simultaneously promote economic growth and prevent the consequences that industrialism had brought in other societies, especially England.' (p. 217)

Carnoy (1974) states the case more bluntly: 'Form schooling is part and parcel of the characteristics of capitalist growth.' (p. 321) The state uses the formal schooling of a skilled labour force as part of the necessary infrastructural provisions of the industrial society. Schooling is a major instrument for fitting people into the hierarchy of the capitalist economy. This also applies to the spread of the Western type schooling to developing countries. The school is an instrument for the maintenance and reproduction of class relationships in society and is not primarily an agent of social mobility and change. It is admitted that schooling in capitalist societies serves as a means of achieving higher status for a '*small percentage* of the urban poor and an even smaller number of rural poor', and even that it can contribute to dissent and original thinking and thereby be a force for societal change. But 'they are by-products of schooling which occur as it attempts to achieve its main function of transmitting the social and economic structure from generation to generation through pupil selection, defining culture and rules, and teaching certain cognitive skills.' (p. 13)

CRITIQUE OF NEO-MARXIST CRITICISM

Are the 'by-products' of schooling as insignificant as has been maintained? Changes in the social composition of enrolment in higher education in Sweden, a capitalist or 'mixed' economy where the overwhelming portion of the means of production is privately owned, could serve as an illustration. In 1950 only 6–7 per cent of the students enrolled in higher education were of working class background. Their parents belonged to the third group in a socio-economic classification system of only three groups. Most parents were wage earners who had primary education only. Group 3 consisted of 50 per cent of the electorate, whereas group 2 (white-collar workers with education usually beyond the primary level) and group 1 (professionals and managers) accounted for 43 and 7 per cent respectively. Socio-economic group 1 in 1950 constituted 7 per cent of the population but included 50 per cent of the university enrolment.

This meant that in 1950 of one hundred young people of working class background only one or two went to university as compared to some 40 in the upper stratum.

By 1969–70, however, 23 per cent of the university enrolment came from socio-economic group 3, whose representation in the electorate had diminished somewhat. The participation rate in higher education among young people of working class background was 10 per cent as compared to some 20 per cent of all young people of university age (*Statistiska Centralbyrån*, 1976).

The over-all picture is therefore one of considerable levelling out between upper and lower status groups in participation in higher education. Can the evidence be interpreted as supporting the notion that the educational system operates as an instrument for reproducing existing class differences and for serving the interest of the ruling class represented by socio-economic group 1? To some extent the interpretation depends on whether the proverbial glass is described as half-empty or half-full. But apart from that, the conclusion rests on somewhat shaky ground. In the first place, the percentage of young people from socio-economic group 3 that went to the university had increased almost tenfold over a 20-year period. Secondly, the main criterion for being assigned to socio-economic group 1 is education. The majority of the students from this group have parents with further education. Most of them are salaried workers employed in public agencies as civil servants and teachers. They are in a true Marxist sense 'workers' who sell their labour. Thirdly, and more importantly, the discrepancy in participation in higher education applies with the same force to formally socialist countries, at least in Eastern Europe, from where enrolment statistics and surveys of educational aspirations began to be available in the 1960s (Sauvy *et al.*, 1973).

The radical critics from the 'New Left' represent a wide spectrum in ideological orientation from anarchism to Marxism. Most of them challenge the traditional liberal view of formal education as an instrument of progress and democracy. The school system in their view is created by the ruling class in order to teach conformity and complacency and to preserve the *status quo.* The 'crisis' that the school of today is undergoing is regarded as a logical result of the failure of society at large.

In her review of a series of publications on the history of American education by the 'revisionists', Diane Ravitch (1977) succinctly sums up how the radical historians view the history of the public school:

First, the school was used by the rich and the middle class as an instrument to manipulate and control the poor and the working class. Second, efforts to extend schooling to greater numbers and to reform the schools were primarily middle-class morality campaigns intended to enhance the coercive power of the school. Third, an essential purpose of the school was to stamp out cultural diversity and to advance homogeneity. Fourth, the idea that upward social mobility might be achieved by children of the poor through schooling was a fable. Fifth, bureaucracy was deliberately selected as the most appropriate structure for perpetuating social stratification by race, sex, and social class. Sixth, a primary function of schooling was to serve the needs of capitalism by instilling appropriate work habits in future workers. Seventh, those liberals and progressives who tried to make the schools better were serving the interests of the status quo. Lastly, reformers and liberal historians of education have been responsible for the American people's failure to understand the true nature and function of schools. (pp. 8–9)

These contentions are challenged by Ravitch on the basis of both logical considerations and historical–empirical evidence. In the first place, the social and economic determinism of dogmatic Marxism easily leads to fallacious reductionism. This applies to the way 'social class' is used as an explanatory concept. When statistics on participation in higher education or on social mobility are presented, parental occupations are usually classified into three categories, upper, middle, and lower class, largely corresponding to professional–managerial, clerical, and manual workers. The finding that the upper class shows a much higher participation rate than the lower class is then taken as support for the contention that the educational system suppresses the working class. Two objections to such an interpretation readily present themselves. Similar, or even greater, differences between 'intelligentsia' and 'functionaries' on the one hand and manual workers on the other are found in formally socialist countries, for instance in the Soviet Union (cf. Rutkewitch, 1969; Sauvy *et al.*, 1973). Thus, they can hardly be mainly explained as an effect of the capitalist system. The neo-Marxist identification of hierarchy in school and work is, as Karabel and Halsey (1977) put it, 'a vast oversimplification'. Secondly, classes are hardly distinct and rigid entities with which 'members' identify themselves. I have pointed out (Husén, 1977a) that in Sweden, for instance, the 'upper' class to a rapidly increasing extent is composed of university-educated people who in terms of salaries show an increasing overlap not only with the middle class but also with manual workers. They are all in the good Marxist sense 'workers' selling their labour to the employers, among whom the State becomes increasingly powerful in terms of both influence and the number of employees.

Katz (1971, p. xviii) sweepingly contends: 'Modern bureaucracy is a bourgeois invention; it represents a crystallization of bourgeois social attitudes.' But the problem then becomes how to account for the excessive bureaucracy in socialist societies in terms of bourgeois values. In the press of Eastern European countries one often finds complaints and castigations of bureaucratic excesses of the same kind as in the Western countries. There is ample evidence to show that bureaucratic tendencies are part and parcel of the development of expanding, complex institutions and organizations.

Another example of excessive reductionism is offered by the description of how public schools were established. They were, according to the dogma, imposed by the ruling class on an unwilling working class and peasantry. There is a kernel of truth in this. Primary schooling in Sweden, for instance, was made mandatory with more support in the estate parliament from the new class of entrepreneurs and part of the nobility than from the representatives of the farmers (who had to carry the costs). But to interpret this as an act of the ruling class to educate docile and disciplined workers is indeed to simplify the matter. In the first place, the clergy, also being a powerful group, was to a large extent opposed to the establishment of a common school simply because it was rightly viewed as an institution that in the long run might affect clerical influence.

Secondly, the dogmatic interpretation assumes not only one single motive behind a policy act but also a clear-cut correspondence between intention and effects. The same liberals who spearheaded mandatory primary schooling were also in the forefront of promoting extension of voting rights and of fighting for local self-government. Those who in England by the early nineteenth century pioneered infant schools were not merely working in their self-interest by helping to establish institutions that took care of children in the age range 2 to 7 whose parents were working long hours in the factories. They had also experienced the social effects of children being left on their own and wanted to cope with these adverse effects of industrialization.

HAS THE SCHOOL THE RIGHT TO 'EDUCATE'?

A stimulating contribution to the debate on the 'proper' functions of the school in modern society has been provided by Carl Bereiter (1973) in his book *Must We Educate?* He does not question the necessity of having an institution that provides basic skills and knowledge. He does question, however, the right of the school to 'educate', to impose on all children the prevailing mode of behaviour and valuation. Such claims are not compatible with the ethos of a free, pluralistic society. The salient feature of the school in modern society is the prerogative of the State to provide an education which leaves no room for young people to try out their own ways and to learn from their own mistakes. The functions of the common school in a democratic society should be twofold: to take care of the children when they are not under the care of the home, and to teach certain basic skills and knowledge, in the first place the three Rs.

The overriding problem in delineating the role of the school is to draw the borderline between public service and public intrusion on the right of the individual to set his own educational goals. Illich and Reimer keep coming back to the notion that in modern society the individuals are manipulated to become like narcomaniacs dependent upon institutions which generate a growing need for their own services and which develop increasingly powerful bureaucracies.

Bereiter's alternative is to provide young people with more freedom to choose their own learning opportunities and to let adult competence-providers, who do not necessarily have to be teachers, play an increasingly important part in their education. Instead of aspiring to be an All-Educator the school has to be reduced to what it was set up to be: an institution that first and foremost provides the basic skills and knowledge with the help of which young people can acquire the additional competence needed in order to get along in adult life.

3

Institutional Schooling: Historical Roots and Evolution

WHAT SHOULD WE MEAN BY A SCHOOL?

THE school as an institution is such an integral part of modern society that it is taken as a forever-given unchangeable entity. However, many salient features of the school of today, such as universality and full-time attendance, have emerged in Europe and North America only during the last hundred years. Both as a place for teaching and as an instrument serving the State, the school has become a powerful institution concomitantly with the development of the industrialized national state. In order to gain useful insights into today's educational dilemmas and problems it is desirable to provide an historical perspective of certain dominant features. How did it happen that primary education became mandatory and universal?

Everett Reimer (1971) defines schools 'as institutions that require full-time attendance of specific age groups in teacher-supervised classrooms for the study of graded curricula'. (p. 35) According to this definition the majority of primary schools by the mid-nineteenth century in Europe, in Sweden for instance, were *not* schools in a real sense.

First, they did not require full-time attendance. The great majority of children in rural areas went to school only for a rather limited number of days per year. Attendance every other day or in alternate semesters or only for a few weeks per year was common practice. During the first decades of compulsory schooling in Sweden, when provision, not attendance, was mandatory, home instruction was regarded as complementary to school instruction (Johansson, 1977). It was understood that basic competence in identifying letters and words should be

provided by instruction at home. These skills were later provided by the junior primary school established some decades
after the passage of the 1842 Primary Education Act in Sweden.

Second, age specifications for school attendance have been
rather stable over time, although age of entry and age of school
leaving were more flexible a century ago. Quite early in the
development of institutional schooling a certain age bracket was
regarded as the one appropriate for primary school attendance,
although child labour laws were often violated by accepting
children for work before completion of primary school.

Third, the model of 'frontal' classroom instruction has become increasingly dominant as classes have become more
homogeneous in age and competence. At the beginning of
institution-building home instruction was, as indicated above,
supposed to precede and complement school instruction. The
monitor system, whereby more advanced pupils taught their
less advanced peers, was a widespread practice in the middle of
the last century in Western and Northern Europe.

Fourth, the graded curriculum in its present form is also a
rather late development. At the outset children of various ages
were taught in the same classroom according to a curriculum
structured in a certain sequence. But the highly elaborate
textbook-guided curriculum had not yet emerged. The struc-
turing of the learning material into a syllabus for each grade or
standard has since then become increasingly prevalent. The
elaborate curriculum is matched by an elaborate system of
marking student progress.

Fifth, the size of the basic unit, the local school house or com-
pound of houses, has grown concomitantly with urbanization
and the consolidation of school districts and/or catchment areas.
The time of the 'little red schoolhouse', which formed a cultural
centre in a society dominated by agriculture, has definitely
passed. In the industrialized countries the typical child of
primary school age some 40 to 50 years ago still went to a school
with an enrolment of less than one hundred students. Secondary
schools with their more specialized curricula necessarily had to
have larger enrolments but were still rather small. Consolidation, urbanization, and the diversification of programmes have
together caused the average enrolment figure to multiply
manifoldly.

Sixth, the size of the system, the number of school units under the jurisdiction of local, regional, and national school administration, and enrolment figures, particularly at the secondary level, have grown dramatically. More children are staying more years in full-time attendance at school. Both teaching and in particular non-teaching staff have increased in relation to the number of students.

Seventh, the objectives of the school have been widened. In addition to imparting certain basic skills and knowledge the school is expected to 'educate', to bring up independent, critical, and responsible citizens ready to exercise their rights and duties as members of a democratic and pluralistic society. But in addition to imparting knowledge and educating the school is also expected to shoulder other responsibilities which are more or less 'extra-curricular' and require the pupils to spend more hours per day in school than before. This, for instance, is the purpose of the SIA-reform in Sweden (SOU, 1974) which extends the responsibilities of the school considerably and consequently lengthens the school day. The custodial care that the school has taken on in a society where both parents to an increasing extent are working outside the home implies extensions to the programmes of health, nutrition, and general caretaking. New categories of personnel, such as psychologists, social workers, nurses, and doctors, have become part of the school staff. Other supportive staff, such as janitors and technicians, has also increased.

Eighth, the increased size of the system and its sub-systems, as well as the complexity of functions, call for increased co-ordination which in its turn means more administrative staff at the local, regional, and state levels. Apart from a justified growth, self-serving empire-building and bureaucratic power-seeking have emerged.

Ninth, supervision has gradually become tighter and operations more uniform, standardized, and rigid. Standardized tests and examinations are instruments by means of which a hierarchy of administrators in a Ministry of Education or a State Department in the last analysis exercises its supervision. Standardized curricula, textbooks, and other mass-produced teaching materials serve the same purpose. Thus, greater uniformity in provisions and standards is achieved.

In these and other respects the school has increasingly become an institution with distinctive features that sets it off from other institutions and from society at large.

THE NEED FOR CUSTODIAL CARE

In industrialized England two new institutions emerged during the first part of the nineteenth century: the Bell–Lancaster system for providing mass elementary instruction with a minimum of teachers to children of primary school age, and infant schools for children from 2 to 7. Parents worked long hours in factories and mines. When legislation limiting child labour was passed in the 1830s—children already having become less useful in industry—there was a strong need for institutions that could take care of them. A private philanthropic movement raised funds that contributed to the establishment of infant schools based on the principle of monitorial teaching.

Carl af Forsell, a Swedish social statistician with liberal views, visited England in 1834 in order to study its social problems and how they were tackled. He was particularly interested in its infant schools. His observations were published under the title *Anteckningar i anledning av en resa till England i slutet av sommaren 1834* (Notes from a Journey to England at the End of the Summer of 1834). He was amazed to find that children even below the age of 5 were able to read and calculate and in some cases had even acquired some historical and geographical knowledge. The children as a rule attended school for three hours in the morning and two to three hours in the afternoon. The parents had to pay a small fee. The rest of the operating costs were provided by private organizations. Forsell believed that the 'education of working-class children should not be provided free of charge, otherwise it would lose its value'. (p. 115)

The teaching of useful skills and knowledge was, however, not the only purpose of these schools. They had two other important aims. 'One is that thereby the children already from the age of 2 by being used to attentiveness, order, obedience, reflection and self-activity by necessity must acquire certain skills in thinking', which in combination with cleanliness and purposeful gymnastic exercises would have a wholesome influence on their future inclinations, thereby laying the foundation of a good education. 'The other circumstance, which perhaps is even more important for the working class, is that, since the children are too small to contribute to their own support or that of their families and require supervision that absorbs the time from adults, responsibility is transferred to the school. Thereby their parents are given better opportunities to increase their wages.' (p. 121)

He refuted the conservative objection against infant schools —that parental care was the most understanding and tender and that institutions of this kind were therefore unnecessary for infants—by maintaining that one should consider the lower level of morality in the working class. All education, not least that provided in institutions, had to be permeated by a Christian spirit. He quoted the Annual Report of the English and Foreign School Society of 1832, which pointed out that 'the time is approaching when England's and any other country's welfare will prevail not because of the scope of its wealth, the extension of its trade or the value of its colonies, but by its education, morality and sound religious principles. May it not be forgotten that every child who gets a Christian education is an insurance of public peace and fortifies the spirit of piety and true virtue which in dangerous times is the only safe protection.' (p. 122)

It is striking to observe that many who promoted the establishment of primary schools tended to use industrial analogies in describing their mode of production and/or processing of the children. It is, however, not necessary to go as far as Michael Katz in *Class, Bureaucracy, and Schools*, who maintains that it was in the 'interest of the ruling class' to increase opportunities for schooling, to widen admission, and to prolong schooling in order to pacify the poor and convey to them the (false) impression of equality of opportunity. Schooling conveys to the poor the impression that they are taken care of. In reality it is the better-off who benefit from the system, Katz contends, because the costs of schooling, which mainly serves an élite, have to be carried by all social strata.

Katz further contends that the strongest force behind the creation of public education in the United States was what in the jargon of today would be called the quest for 'law and order'. The implicit, and sometimes even explicit, goal was to socialize the urban poor and reduce the expenditures caused by welfare and crime. Despite evidence to the contrary, faith in the school as an instrument for coping with social problems has prevailed, which he thinks is 'one of the great puzzles of American thought'. He offers the following explanation:

An official ideology that emphasizes the importance of free enterprise and shuns state intervention has limited alternatives with which to approach major social problems, such as poverty. Massive income redistribution or broad-scale intervention in the economy has generally not been acceptable. Education, on the other hand, has appeared to be an immediate and effective solution to social problems. There is a surface logic, which remains immensely appealing: Equipping children with appropriate skills and attitudes can cause the problem of unemployment and poverty to disappear. The illnesses of society become diagnosed as simply a lack of education, and the prescription for reform becomes more education. (p. 109)

In his study of educational reform in mid-nineteenth century Massachusetts Katz (1968) attempts to show that the reform movement for universal primary schooling inspired by Horace Mann was a massive attempt to establish better social control. The masses could thereby become 'orderly, moral and tractable'. He maintains that by 1880 the system of public education had essentially acquired the characteristics that have since then prevailed. In pursuing further his studies on the emergence of universal primary education, Katz came to the conclusion that 'the purpose has been, basically, the inculcation of attitudes that reflect dominant social and industrial values; the structure has been bureaucracy.' (Katz, 1971, p. XVIII.)

The same interpretation is advanced by Bowles and Gintis in several studies where they try to show, even with empirical data, that the main function of the school today is to make students docile and disciplined so as to fit into the hierarchical structure of today's working life (see, e.g., Bowles and Gintis, 1973; Bowles, 1971).

But this is a highly simplified description of a process behind which there is a complicated pattern of forces. It was no doubt in the self-interest of the new class of proprietors and entrepreneurs to set up an institution that could take care of the children and inculcate useful skills while their parents worked long hours in the factories. We have ample evidence to show for instance that the State Lutheran Church in some countries was a strong force in promoting literacy, though not necessarily in the promotion of an institutionalized form of schooling. The clergy in Sweden, for instance, was deeply divided when legislation on compulsory primary education was prepared in the 1830s and early 1840s. However, the promotion of a common basic school in Europe was strongly supported by liberal pioneers on the basis of motives of participation in the democratic process of local government and of greater equality of opportunity.

The role of bureaucracy as an instrument for enforcing compulsory education to 'pacify' the masses and make them more docile would appear to be similar in both capitalist and socialist systems. The state bureaucracy in both systems is similar enough to justify the question of whether or not the technological civilization creates its own conditions beyond capitalism and socialism. I shall come back to this problem in Chapter 7 when dealing with the role of bureaucracy in modern school systems.

As has been demonstrated by means of the records of the annual examinations conducted by the parish priests in Sweden since the end of the seventeenth century, the ability to read the Scriptures increased slowly in a linear fashion over the period from 1700 until the 1840s (Johansson, 1973 and 1977). There was some acceleration during the early part of the nineteenth century when, through the private initiative of owners of estates, big enterprises, and clergymen, schools were founded. Among liberal representatives of the new class of entrepreneurs there was a strong movement for establishing in the industrial areas infant schools of the type set up in England for the age range 2 to 7. As was indicated by Carl af Forsell, the fact that the great majority of adults was able to read (but not to write) was due mainly to the 'push' effect of the annual examinations given by the clergy and the instruction provided in the home, as a rule by the mother. Home instruction was still a major vehicle for literacy in Sweden even after the passing of the 1842 Primary Education Act. One prominent Swedish educator, Bishop C. A. Agardh, moved in Parliament the establishment of so-called home instruction schools which the children, depending upon the local circumstances, could attend once or twice a week in order to be given homework assignments on which the teacher could examine them the next time they came to school.

Of the four estates (nobility, clergy, burghers, farmers), the farmers offered the greatest resistance to compulsory provision of primary schooling, which was a traumatic experience for the more liberal and progressive members of the estate. The arguments advanced against the Bill were the following. (1) The Bill imposed the provisions for at least one primary school in each parish. The costs of teacher salaries and of construction and maintenance of the school building had to be carried by the parishioners themselves. The State had only to establish and support Normal Schools in each province in order to provide the schools with competent teachers. (2) Since the poor section of the peasantry, tenant farmers and crofters, needed their children's labour, they resented their being away from home for a substantial part of the week. As primary schools developed, full-time school attendance was an exception in the rural areas well into the twentieth century. (3) It seemed inappropriate to give girls the same school education as boys. Among the peasantry at that time everybody was required to read the Scriptures. The girls, as opposed to the boys, were not expected to be able to write, nor were they expected to learn history and geography which according to the Bill were included in the primary school curriculum.

In order to free the children for work at home most members of the Parliament representing farmers were in favour of a reduced curriculum. The strongest support in the Parliament for the Bill was found in the estate of proprietors and entrepreneurs, many of whom had at their own initiative established schools close to factories. Next to the proprietors, the house of nobility took the most positive attitude towards the new Bill.

DEVELOPMENT OF LITERACY IN NINETEENTH-CENTURY SWEDEN

Carl af Forsell noted with dismay in an earlier book *Statistik över Sverige* (Statistics About Sweden) 1833, that the lower classes in Sweden were assumed by foreign visitors to be completely illiterate. He points out that this was an entirely false conception. The overwhelming majority was able to read. Those who were not able to read the Scriptures ran the risk of not being admitted to the Last Supper and not being permitted to marry. He goes on to say that even if the cabins of the tenant farms or peasants bore witness to extreme poverty, one could in most cases find a Bible, a Book of Hymns, and other religious literature. He refers to the British Lord Chancellor, who pointed out in Parliament in 1816 that many thousand couples in Manchester who had been married during six years preceding 1816 were not even able to write their own names and that in France only 38 per cent of the young men called up for military service were able to read.

Egil Johansson (1977), who has conducted extensive studies of how Sweden became literate by utilizing the unique source material consisting of records from catechism examinations, has identified three reasons why the development of literacy differed in Sweden from most of continental Europe and England.

(1) There was a strong religious and political 'push'. The Church Law of 1686 had made reading competence mandatory for marriage and participation in church ceremonies, such as the Last Supper. The parish priest examined all adults regularly, usually once a year, with regard to literacy and mastery of the Scriptures. In many parishes the examinees were given graded marks.

(2) The development of reading ability was far ahead of the ability to write. By mid-1800 the great majority of adults was able to read, whereas only a minority could write.

(3) The literacy campaign was launched almost entirely without resort to formal schooling. In the last analysis the parents had the responsibility of seeing to it that the children learned to read, and the parents were controlled by the clergy. The overwhelming majority had achieved literacy in reading long before provisions for elementary schooling were made compulsory by legislation in all the parishes. Still some 25–30 years later about one-fifth to one-third of all children were taught at home, and children who entered elementary school were expected to have acquired some basic reading skills at home. A particular 'junior' elementary school covering two years was not established until well into the 1850s.

Johansson points out that two main forces can be traced behind the development of literacy in protestant Europe. On the one side there was, as indicated above, the 'push' exerted by religious control. On the other side was the 'pull' exerted by

social and economic forces concomitant with incipient industrialization. In his book *Literacy and Development in the West*
Cippola (1969) estimates that by 1700 between 35 and 45 per
cent of the adults in protestant Europe were literate. Catechism
and the Book of Hymns were the most common books. Reading
competence was imparted under strong social pressure both
vertically and horizontally. The control exercised by the parish
priests was of great importance as well as the teaching done at
home or—in some instances before the 1840s—by schoolmasters.

The development of writing literacy cannot, with few exceptions, be studied in the catechization records. Johansson shows
that in eight parishes in the province of Scania in 1750, where
records on writing competence are available, 80 to 90 per cent
were literate in reading but only 10 to 25 per cent in writing.
This observation has important implications for today's developing countries. Almost universal competence in reading can be
achieved, given adequate motivation, in a pre-industrial society
without formal schooling.

Some observations on the development of literacy in a few
other European countries should be added. There we have no
catechization records, only statistics pertaining to frequency of
signatures in connection with marriage ceremonies, examinations of military recruits, and census data. Reading and writing
literacy in these countries tends to develop simultaneously and
not with the time lag for writing ability observed in the Scandinavian countries. Around 1850 to 1880 about half the adult
population in France could read as well as write their names;
according to census data around 1900 some 20–25 per cent
were still not able to read and write.

In England the indicators of literacy are signatures on marriage documents and the assessment of the reading ability of
convicts. Between 1850 and 1870 some 60 per cent of the bride-
grooms and 35–45 per cent of the brides were able to sign their
names. This increased to more than 90 per cent by 1900. Reading literacy among convicts increased from 50–60 per cent in
1850 to 70–80 per cent by the end of the century.

The conception that formal schooling is the only alternative
when it comes to imparting literacy is refuted by the development in the Scandinavian countries. Well into the latter part of
the nineteenth century Sweden was a pre-industrial and poor

country. The majority of adult population was literate before the introduction of formal schooling for which universal provision was made by the Primary School Act of 1842.

Studies of how Europe (Leschinsky and Roeder, 1976) and North America (Lockridge, 1974) became literate can teach important lessons to those who plan for literacy in the Third World. The model of formal schooling, as it had developed well into this century, has been exported to countries whose social and economic conditions differ profoundly from those in Europe of the nineteenth century.

4

Recent Changes and Trends

INSTITUTIONAL CHANGES—AN OVERVIEW

FOR the benefit of subsequent analyses I shall in the present chapter review what has happened on the educational scene over the last few decades and try to identify some salient trends and tendencies. Such an exercise will broaden our perspective and hopefully yield a general notion of the direction in which the school as an institution is moving. The tendencies identified will be dealt with under ten main points. But as a background to the attempt to identify salient changes within the school system it would be useful in the first place to deal briefly with some changes that have occurred in what Cremin (1976) refers to as the 'ecology of education'.

It should be strongly underlined that education cannot be identified with formal schooling only and that it does not occur in a socio-economic vacuum. Formal education is related to various other educational institutions, such as the family, whose role has changed considerably. The family's contribution to the outcomes of schooling has been the central focus of interest among educational researchers and policy makers since the early 1960s, when ideas about compensatory education began to emerge on both sides of the Atlantic (Leichter, 1974). Cremin draws our attention to 'parents, peers, siblings, and friends, as well as families, churches, synagogues, libraries, museums, summer camps, benevolent societies, agricultural fairs, settlement houses, factories, radio stations, and television networks'. (p. 29) These institutions relate to each other in what he calls 'configurations of education'. The educational institutions and configurations have to be viewed in relation to each other and to the larger society that sustains education and that is in turn affected by it.

Profound changes in the composition of the family have taken place in recent years in many industrialized countries, which have had strong repercussions on its educative functions. In the first place, the number of children per family has been going down, a decline that has been particularly drastic since the mid-1960s, when the Pill began to have an impact. The majority of families has only one or two children. Closely related to this is the increase in the number of working mothers. For example, in 1955 in the City of Stockholm only about 15 per cent of married women with children of school age had full-time jobs outside the home. Two decades later their number had increased to some 50 per cent. There has also been a dramatic increase in the number of single-parent families.

The educative effects of these changes in the structure and functions of the family should be examined with particular reference to their impact on the role of the school. The broadened tasks of the school, such as supervising children for a prolonged part of the day, as recently enacted by the reform of the 'inner work' in Sweden, are undoubtedly a response to the new family conditions. The setting up of day-care centres, nursery schools, and kindergartens has been given top priority in the welfare policy of many countries.

The following salient changes that affect the school as an institution have been identified:

(1) Enrolment at the secondary and tertiary levels went through an exponential increase in the 1950s and 1960s after a long period of slow, linear growth. The phrase *'educational explosion'* was coined to characterize the situation. More young people tended to stay an increasing number of years in school. But a dramatic growth has also taken place in adult education, where provisions have been made for those who have been employed for several years to 'go back to school' in order to upgrade their formal education as well as gain specific, work-related competencies. In addition, correspondence courses, evening classes, study circles, and on-the-job training courses have expanded. Legislation has been passed with provisions for study leave and financial assistance. In some European countries and in the United States the 'explosion' of adult participation in educative activities has been even more

significant than that among young people of school age.

(2) The highly industrialized, and even more so the post-industrial, society tends to become increasingly *meritocratic*. It can be aphoristically put this way: educated talent is contemporary society's substitute for family background and inherited wealth. The safest and most inflation-proof investment parents can make is in the education of their children. The meritocratic problem cuts across quite different social and economic orders (Husén, 1974b). The fact that the number of places at the secondary level has been increased to make schooling at that level practically universal and that a rapidly increasing number are entering tertiary education does not mean that competition for access has been removed or even reduced. On the contrary, the greater the number of people climbing to the top of the ladder of formal education, the higher the *formal* competition tends to move. At the same time, however, the repercussions downward in the form of *real* competition are considerable. To take one example: when conducting the international evaluation study of mathematics in the mid-1960s (Husén, 1967) we found that Japan offered opportunities for formal education up to the age of eighteen to a far greater proportion of the relevant age groups than any European country. About two-thirds of the 17–18-year-olds in Japan were in full-time schooling as compared to only 10–30 per cent in Western Europe. One might infer from this that the scrambling for marks and jostling for entry to the next level in the system would be alien to the Japanese system. But nothing could be further from reality, as has been shown by a study by Teichler (1976) with the significant title *Das Dilemma der modernen Bildungsgesellschaft* (The Dilemma of the Modern Learning Society). In the first place, selection for entry to good universities is very tough. The extremely keen competition makes the parents in Japan go out of their way to get their children into the 'right' secondary school in the belief that being from that school will put them on the inside track for getting into a prestigious university. But in order to get into the 'right' secondary school one has to be admitted to the 'right' primary school—and even into the 'right' pre-primary institution.

(3) Education (and research) since the beginning of the

1960s has been conceived of as a major *contributor to economic growth*. Economists have tried to assess the rate-of-return to the individual and society that education yields. Investment in human capital has begun to be regarded as a necessary prerequisite to sustaining the high-level technology of our present-day society. A certain level of competence with regard to communication skills, numeracy, and general knowledge is indispensable for the coping power of an individual in such a complex society. Awareness of the strategic role played by education in individual career development, but also the increased 'consumption' of education that has been an outcome of improved standards of living, has led to the allocation of larger and larger slices of the public resources to education, research, and development.

No wonder, then, that the 'knowledge industry' has increased tremendously during recent decades. Machlup (1962) defines the knowledge industry as education, research and development, media of communication, information, and servicing. According to a study conducted by Machlup (1973) on the basis of the 1970 U.S. Census data, the growth rate of that industry was 9 per cent per year from 1958 to 1970. In 1958, formal education accounted for 44 per cent of the total output of the knowledge industry which corresponded to 13 per cent of the GNP. Since 1958 the enrolment has increased tremendously. For example, in 1970 60 per cent of the 18–21-year-olds were in higher education as compared with only 34 per cent in 1960. Furthermore, since the unit cost (per student and year) has gone up considerably, one can expect the growth of expenditures in education to be considerably higher than the 9 per cent per year for the entire knowledge industry.

(4) The '*knowledge explosion*' is an expression coined to describe the swelling of research under increasingly specialized conditions. The documented knowledge in scientific journals and monographs grows exponentially, so that in many areas the output in terms of the number of research reports doubles every five to ten years. Specialization and the role that research plays in the transformation of society today make it increasingly difficult for the man in the street either to absorb and interpret what the specialists (both the researchers who produce the knowledge and the technologists who apply it) are up to, or to assess the

impact of their work on the present and especially on the future society. The individual at the grassroots level has the uneasy feeling of being in the hands of the technocrats.

(5) Young people today spend their teens at school with *few contacts with adults and the world of work.* The school made compulsory in most countries in Western Europe by the mid-nineteenth century did not until the mid-twentieth century extend its purview beyond the age of twelve to fourteen. As late as the 1930s the overwhelming majority of young people in these countries left school at the beginning of their teens. Today, the great majority is in full-time schooling during the entire teenage span. This fact alone signifies a revolution in the social role of these age groups. Instead of performing an adult role the young person of secondary school age finds himself treated in essentially the same way as he was in the elementary school. In modern society physiological puberty is followed by a prolonged social and psychological puberty, a period of preparation for the adult role in society, a role far more complicated than the one played in the subsistence economy where the family was the main educational agent. The problem of a prolonged psychological puberty has become exacerbated by the fact that today's teenagers reach physiological puberty almost two years earlier than at the turn of the century. Today young people sit in school all those years during which their age-mates at the beginning of the century were learning adult roles outside the school walls. This paradox of superimposed childlike and adult roles poses formidable problems for educators.

The full scope and the educational policy implications of these problems, particularly at the secondary level, have only been grasped in recent years. I shall devote a separate chapter (Chapter 8) to them later in this book. Suffice it to point out here that the issues that will dominate present and future teen-age education can be summed up in two words: participation and relevance. They relate both to what happens in school and its bearing on the world of work. We are faced here with a dilemma. On the one hand, young people want to take on adult roles and participate in the world of work, but on the other hand the labour market cannot absorb men and women lacking a broad general education. In order to achieve greater participation and meaningfulness in education one has to find ways of conferring adult responsibilities on young people in the larger societal context and particularly in the working community.

(6) *The school no longer has a monopoly on knowledge transmission.* When compulsory elementary schooling was introduced in Western Europe in the mid-nineteenth century, its principal duties were to inculcate the three Rs and the ethical conduct conveyed by the Scriptures. It was a school operating in a world of monolithic values, in which home and school were reinforcing each other as educational agents. Mass media have tremendously enlarged the horizon of experience: once confined to the four walls of the home or the home town, that horizon now takes in the whole world. In a way quite different from earlier generations, today's young people are globally minded, due in no small measure to the remarkable facility of television to convey concrete impressions (even if no more than glimpses) of events as they unfold, including atrocities of war and misery in the Third World. Young people growing up today are exposed as much to emanations from the magic cathode-ray tube as to the pronouncements of teachers who stand before them in the classroom. In fact, in many countries TV sets are to be found in almost one hundred per cent of the homes and the viewing that takes place covers about the same amount of time as school attendance.

(7) *Institutional schooling tends to be intermittently extended to the entire life-span.* Up till now, institutional schooling has been limited to a narrow age span, say from 5–6 to 17–18 years of age. During that time its students have been more or less separated, not to say segregated, from the surrounding society, above all from the world of work. Typically enough, up to the 1950s the business community, trade unions, and employer organizations in most European countries hardly paid any attention to school matters. The school was conceived largely on the basis of the principle that a certain part of early life had to be devoted entirely to learning what the adult 'needs to know'. The young were then supposed to ingest the fare of knowledge and skills that would nourish them for the rest of their lives. This principle is unworkable in a rapidly changing technological society, in which any kind of knowledge and competence, not least in the vocational sphere, tends to get out-of-date rapidly. The individual has to keep on learning—and

eventually unlearning—in order to cope with the changes
thrown up by technology and by the knowledge industry. An
important corollary to this is a displacement of the educational
objectives themselves, with emphasis shifting from the inculcation of specific knowledge or competencies toward acquiring
skills which have a broad range of applications in unforeseen
and not yet 'invented' situations.

(8) *The role of the teacher is changing.* The new technology—as
embodied in radio and T V sets, sound and videotape recorders,
not to mention computers—has opened up new vistas in instruction. The teacher has become less of a transmitter or communi-
cator of knowledge and more of a planner of learning
opportunities and a monitor of individual learning progress.
Since staffing costs are by far the largest in the school's operating budget, one has to economize with the teacher's time in
order to curb the steeply rising expenditures. The central purpose in trying to control the cost increase must be to take a hard
look at what teacher tasks are essential in the teaching–learning
process, such as maintaining contact with and guiding the
students, both individually and in small groups.

A decade ago the hopes were high for what might be achieved
by audio-visual teaching aids in terms of saving teacher time.
However, one cannot stress strongly enough that the school is
not a factory and that teachers are *not* replaceable by machines
or other technological devices. (In cases where a replacement is
justifiable, the circumstances are, indeed, abnormal!)

The 'efficiencies' aspired to in the system can be gained by
other measures. A strong case can be argued for reducing the
number of teacher-led work periods per week in the secondary
school. In place of the thirty-to-forty-period week of conventional classroom work, in most countries dominated by 'frontal
instruction' it may be feasible to reduce the number to twenty
periods, with provision for the teacher's active participation
when his physical presence is necessary. The amount of independent learning time for the students would increase
correspondingly.

(9) During a period of a few decades the *school units have
become increasingly larger* in all industrialized countries, particularly at the secondary level, where a sufficient range of course
offerings implies a minimum number of specialist teachers and

hence a minimum number of classes at each grade level. In 1970–71, the International Association for the Evaluation of Educational Achievement sampled schools at the primary and secondary levels in some twenty countries. The typical primary school student in a developed country goes to a school with an enrolment of about 400, and the typical secondary student to a school with about 750 (Passow *et al.*, 1976). The 'little red schoolhouse' of the countryside has disappeared in a sweeping merger process.

The expansion of the educational system also extends to its *organizational machinery*. Education takes place within the framework of increasingly larger administrative units, often created under the (often mistaken) belief in economy of size. The hierarchy of decision-makers has grown, with the convergence of more power to the summit and the proliferation of time-consuming channels for the transaction of business. In spite of assurances to the contrary in an era when participation and grassroots involvement are 'in'-words, increased centralization is a *fait accompli*, even at the level of local school administration. As more links are inserted in the hierarchical chain and the direct contacts between decision-makers and the classrooms diminish, formalism becomes magnified, thereby diverting attention from the substance of education.

Traditional models of bureaucratic administration in education have recently been brought into question (Pusey, 1976). The crucial issue is to what extent bureaucratic steering is compatible with the educative functions which the schools and the teachers are supposed to fulfil.

(10) A list of current tendencies in today's school would be incomplete if we did not include the so-called *generation gap*. Much could no doubt be said about this, for we are here confronted with what Nietzsche once referred to as 'a re-evaluation of all values'. James Coleman (1961) drew our attention to the problem by his studies of the value climate in American high schools. The dominant influence of the peer culture and identification with the values cherished in the peer group brought him to talk about an 'adolescent society' as separate from the society at large, that of adults. The central thesis in the report, *Youth: Transition to Adulthood* (Coleman *et al.*, 1974), submitted by the panel that he chaired, is that the school shares the task of

socialization with the family and the peer group. 'Our basic premise is that the school system, as now constituted, offers an incomplete context for the accomplishment of many important facets of maturation. The school has been well designed to provide some kinds of training, but by virtue of that fact, is inherently ill-suited for other tasks essential to the creation of adults.' (p. 2)

The existence of a generation gap has been questioned by others who have surveyed groups of teenagers in Europe and North America (see, e.g., Andersson, 1969). It has been maintained that those who turn against time-honoured values are young people who have by and large grown up under favourable material circumstances and whose parents have 'made it'. They oppose the middle-class puritan work ethic, the 'sweat-it-out philosophy' that the parental generation is said to represent. The young ones are asking themselves whether the material results of the nine-to-five drudgery are worth the price. We shall take up these problems in more depth in Chapter 8.

DEMOGRAPHIC AND ENROLMENT TRENDS IN HIGHLY INDUSTRIALIZED COUNTRIES

Much of the 'crisis' in education is related to unexpected changes in birth rates, participation rates in schooling, and economic climate. We therefore found it worthwhile to venture an attempt to illustrate statistically some salient trends in European and American education. There are three main sources of statistical information about national systems of education available for such an exercise: UNESCO (1975), OECD (1975), and the World Bank (IBRD, 1976). Since we were interested primarily in the highly industrialized countries, we were confined mainly to the information available from OECD. It would obviously have been of great interest to include some Eastern European countries; the task of collating this material and rendering the data comparable was, however, beyond the scope of the resources available for this project.

Since the comparisons were limited to Europe and North America, we were left with sixteen OECD nations. The countries are listed in Table 1, with the duration of formal schooling as well as the rates of increase in *per capita* income in the period

1960 to 1970. They show certain common demographic features. Population growth rates are uniformly low. Most countries are densely populated. All have high life expectancies at birth. Roughly 70 per cent of their populations live in urban centres. There are uniformly high levels of publicly supported education. The *per capita* income is high and increased substantially during the 1960s. They are all on the downward trend in terms of fertility to the extent of being close to replacement level. Birth rates in some countries have already fallen below that level.

TABLE I

Duration of Formal Schooling and Increase in per capita
Incomes 1960–70

Country	Duration of Compulsory Schooling (in years) 1974	Average no. Years of Formal Schooling 1970	Percentage Increase in *per capita* Income 1960–70
Austria	9	11·6	117
Belgium	8	14·5	115
Canada	9–10	12·8	81
Denmark	9	11·4	141
Finland	8–9	11·4	100
France	10	14·3	112
Germany (FRG)	9	11·4	127
Ireland	9	12·8	104
Italy	8	10·1	153
Luxembourg	9	12·2	95
Netherlands	9	13·5	154
Norway	9	12·1	125
Sweden	9	12·9	121
Switzerland	8–9	12·1	107
United Kingdom	11	12·3	17
United States	10	14·8	68

Source: UNESCO (1974); OECD (1974).

Before commenting on enrolment trends and participation rates in school education it would be useful to study the demographic determinants of enrolment and the 'shockwave' effects of (often unexpected) changes in birth rates, such as the 'baby boom' after the Second World War. The first-order effect is of course the number of children who enter school after 5–7 years. Second-order effects pertain to the demand for classrooms and teachers. One could advance several explanations why planning and policy making have notoriously failed to translate information gleaned from simple demography into planned action. To be sure, one factor of great importance is the short cycle of political office. Short-term action is preferred, and once it has gained momentum it is difficult to stop it, even if information conducive to more adequate planning and corrective action is available.

The following example is typical. A peak in absolute birthrate occurred in Sweden in the early twenties with a sharp drop in the following years until the early 1930s when a new slow upsurge began. The increase was of the order of 50 per cent by 1944, when a slow drop began. Evidently these fluctuations had affected the demand for primary school teachers. Thus, a Royal Commission appointed in the early 1930s advanced recommendations about the intake of students to primary-school teacher-training institutions. Rather drastic cuts were recommended that by and large would follow the decline in birth rate. The ensuing legislation followed the recommendations. The last teacher-training colleges that the Parliament decided to shut down closed shortly before the new peak in birth rate occurred. A few years later a crash programme for the establishment of new teacher-training institutions had to be launched in order to meet the rapidly rising demand for primary school teachers!

It is, indeed, difficult to make demographic predictions on the basis of projected birth rates. In the last thirty years demographers have been caught off guard on two occasions. Firstly, the post-war 'baby boom' came as a surprise. Secondly, the general decline in birth rates in the late 1960s—the Germans refer to it as the *Pillenknick*—was similarly not anticipated.

Demographic changes in addition tend to have third-order effects on the labour market in a society where the teaching profession represents a high proportion of skilled labour. In the United States, for example, for every hundred children under five in 1966 there were seventy-seven in 1976. An obvious

effect has been a considerable drop in the construction of classrooms, which has also been affected by the financial squeeze.
Teacher demand, however, lacks the 'elasticity' of consumer
goods. This is reflected in the fact that during the period 1961–2
to 1971–2 the over-all teacher force in the United States increased by 46 per cent. The teacher surplus seemingly hit the
teacher training institutions by surprise in the early 1970s, when
some 40 per cent of the students at universities and colleges
were heading for the teaching profession (Freeman, 1976).
Recently, a great many college graduates with teaching certificates have been unable to find employment in school teaching.
In England twenty teacher training colleges according to recent
decisions will be closed. This development means that an army
of college graduates is going to line up for employment in other
sectors of the high qualification job market. Demographic
changes further affect the promotion prospects among teachers.
Since the upper echelons of the promotion ladder have been
filled up by relatively young people during the boom years,
promotion becomes blocked for new generations.

School enrolment depends on two main factors, both difficult
to predict: birth rates and participation rates. Demographic
studies can, of course, predict with a high level of precision the
absolute number of children (already born) who are eligible for
education at a certain age level. But the number of children not
yet born and the subsequent demand for a public service, such
as education, is highly subject to changes in values and aspirations. These are determined by the economic and social experiences of individuals which can vary considerably from age
group to age group.

The birth rate during the 'baby boom' years of the 1950s and
early 1960s notwithstanding, the demographic factors were *not*
the most important determinants of secondary school enrolment but rather the demand for *participation*. Some countries
experienced what has been labelled a revolution of rising expectations, partly as a result of reform that broadened the
opportunities for further education beyond the mandatory
minimum of elementary schooling. In the 1950s, when comprehensive nine-year schools were established in Sweden on a pilot
basis (to a large extent in areas which so far had had poor or no
provisions for secondary education) about one-third of the

students in grades 7 through 9 opted for the 'academic' programme with two foreign languages. This was used as an
indicative figure for the country as a whole when planning the
capacity of the various programmes and the demand for
specialized teachers. This turned out to be a gross under-
estimation. Soon after the 1962 Education Act had gone into
effect about twice as many as projected, that is to say about
60 per cent, opted for the two-language programme. This reflected a tremendous growth in expectations, when secondary
education became available to all.

Table 2 and Figures 2 and 3 present in condensed form relevant demographic information collated from the OECD
countries.

We have also collated information on enrolment trends in the
same countries. Certain caveats are in order here. Information
on private systems may be either incomplete or lacking altogether. There is an incentive in some countries to report regis-

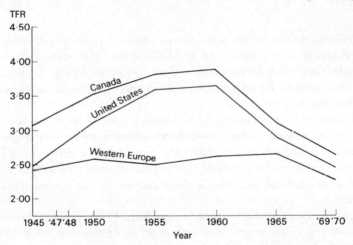

FIG. 2 Total Fertility Rates (TFR)—North American/Western European
Comparisons.

Source: Adapted from Berelson (1974, p. 4).
    The total fertility rate (TFR) is a measure of the average number of
children a woman would have if she experienced the fertility of a cross-
section of women at the time of measurement—that is, a rough approxima-
tion of completed family size. Note that replacement for most countries is
between 2·1 and 2·2.

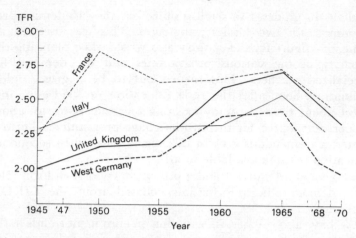

FIG. 3   Total Fertility Rates (TFR)—Selected Western European Countries.

Source: Adapted from Berelson (1974, p. 5).

tration at a time when attendance shows a peak in order to be in a favourable position in qualifying for operational grants. Finally, it should be noted that the enrolment figures presented do not include certain out-of-school schemes, such as evening classes for adults.

It should be kept in mind that even correct enrolment figures do not accurately reflect the volume of pedagogical exposure or learning activities, since there are considerable differences between countries in terms of the annual number of school days and instructional periods. This is shown for nine countries in Table 3.

On the basis of statistics obtained from O E C D we have been able to get an overview of the changes in enrolment since 1960, presented in Table 4. The increase in enrolment is measured by growth indices where the 1965 enrolment is set at 100. The most dramatic increase has occurred at the secondary level, where the enrolment in more than half the countries studied has grown by more than 50 per cent. This occurred during a period when fertility rates were declining and when the shortage of secondary school teachers forced the teacher training institutions to expand their programmes considerably.

TABLE 2

Live Birth Rates (1940-1974) and Fertility Rates (1950-1974) for Sample Countries

Country	Population 1974 ('000)	Birth Rate 1940	1950	1960	1965	1970	1974	Fertility Rate 1950	1960	1965	1970	1974
Austria	7,528	21·8	15·6	17·6	17·9	15·2	12·8	n.a.	62·9	70·7	61·7	48·9
Belgium	9,804	13·6	16·9	17·4	16·4	14·7	12·6	59·3	64·6	65·4	64·0	53·2
Canada	22,479	21·5	27·1	27·5	21·4	17·4	15·5	92·2	95·7	75·6	59·7	51·6
Denmark	5,045	18·3	18·6	16·3	18·0	14·4	14·2	65·3	58·4	63·4	56·4	56·3
Finland	4,682	17·8	24·5	18·9	17·0	14·0	13·3	84·2	63·5	61·3	53·0	45·3
France	52,507	14·0	20·7	18·4	17·6	16·8	15·2	73·3	70·1	68·6	61·0	61·6
Germany	62,041	20·0	16·5	17·6	17·9	13·4	10·1	52·2	58·0	67·9	59·9	37·5
Ireland	3,086	19·1	21·3	21·1	22·2	21·8	23·3	58·0	81·3	81·3	82·6	87·6
Italy	55,361	23·5	19·6	18·4	19·2	16·8	15·7	78·2	59·5	63·3	60·7	57·9
Luxembourg	342	13·4	14·8	15·6	15·6	13·2	11·5	n.a.	56·5	69·3	49·0	38·6
Netherlands	13,541	20·8	22·7	21·3	19·9	18·3	13·8	48·8	75·3	73·9	68·6	51·4
Norway	3,987	16·1	19·1	18·0	17·5	16·6	14·9	78·3	65·5	64·6	67·4	60·0
Sweden	8,161	15·1	16·4	14·1	15·9	13·7	13·4	67·0	51·3	54·7	51·4	52·3
Switzerland	6,481	15·2	18·1	17·7	18·7	15·8	12·9	62·2	61·8	69·7	59·5	46·0
United Kingdom	54,421	14·6	16·3	16·8	18·1	16·3	13·9	55·5	61·3	69·8	62·0	53·4
United States	211,909	17·9	23·5	24·1	19·4	18·3	15·0	81·1	86·1	75·6	61·6	50·8

Source: United Nations, Demographic Year Books. Live birth rates are the number of live births reported for a calendar year per 1,000 persons at the mid-point of the year. Fertility rates are the number of births reported in the calendar year per 1,000 female population aged 10-49 years at the mid-point of the year in question.
Note that the countries in the sample include 48 per cent of the population of the developed world.

TABLE 3

Differences in Instructional Time Per Day and Per Year at
Elementary and School Levels in Nine Countries

	Primary Level			Secondary Level		
	Instruc- tional hours per day	Instruc- tional days per year	Instruc- tional hours per year	Instruc- tional hours per day	Instruc- tional days per year	Instruc- tional hours per year
Belgium	4·2	200	840	5·6	200	1,120
Finland	4·0	200	800	6·0	194	1,164
France	5·4	170	918	5·0	155	775
Germany	3·3	230	759	4·0	230	920
Italy	5·0	175	875	5·8	195	1,131
Netherlands	5·2	200	1,040	5·6	200	1,120
Sweden	5·4	180	972	6·0	180	1,080
United Kingdom	5·0	180	900	5·0	180	900
United States	5·0	180	900	5·0	180	900

Source: Adapted from Passow *et al.* (1976, p. 262).

The striking upward trend in secondary school enrolment is
in most countries a result much more of the rapid increase in
participation rate than in the birth rate. This is shown in
Table 5 where we present the percentage of those particular age
brackets which is enrolled in secondary education.

COST DEVELOPMENT TRENDS

Public expenditures on education as a percentage of the Gross
National Product from 1920 to 1974 form an interesting series.
The figures presented here for illustrative purposes are from a
1976 report by the Swedish Central Bureau of Statistics
(*Statistiska Centralbyrån*, 1976).

1920	1·8 per cent		
1930	2·5 ,, ,,	1920–30	+0·7
1940	2·6 ,, ,,	1930–40	+0·1
1950	3·0 ,, ,,	1940–50	+0·4
1960	4·4 ,, ,,	1950–60	+1·4
1965	5·2 ,, ,,		

TABLE 4

Enrolments and Growth Indices in Elementary and Secondary Schooling

Country	Ages of Compulsory Schooling 1974	Elementary School Enrolment Growth Indices (1965 = 100)				per cent change 1965–75	Secondary School Enrolment Growth Indices (1965 = 100)				per cent change 1960–74	per cent change 1970–74
		1960	1965	1970	1975		1960	1965	1970	1974		
Austria	6–15	85	100	113	107	7·4	102	100	145	163	59·2	18
Belgium	6–14	94	100	102	95	−5·2	82	100	113	125	53·3	12
Canada	6/7–15/16	90	100	102	95	6·0	71	100	127	130	82·7	3
Denmark	7–16	—	100	102	114	13·8	—	100	106	101	—	−5
Finland	7–16	118	100	84	89	−10·8	82	100	118	118	42·3	0
France	6–16	101	100	99	95	−1·4	80	100	116	125	56·8	9
Germany	6–15	90	100	115	120	20·0	93	100	128	151	63·1	23
Ireland	6–15	93	100	102	106	5·7	—	100	145	180	—	35
Italy	6–14	97	100	108	108	8·0	72	100	125	150	109·5	25
Luxembourg	6–15	32	100	111	111	0·0	90	100	155	155	72·2	0
Netherlands	6/7–15	100	100	103	103	2·8	89	100	117	141	58·4	24
Norway	7–16	104	100	94	94	−6·1	—	100	127	138	—	11
Sweden	7–16	112	100	100	107	7·5	78	100	110	106	36·4	−4
Switzerland	6/7–14/16	100	100	105	—	—	80	100	125	104	—	−4
United Kingdom	5–16	96	100	112	112	12·4	—	100	112	135	—	23
United States	6/7–16/18	90	100	100	92	−7·6	80	100	112	116	43·8	4

Source: OECD (1974). The tables from the OECD, Education Statistics Yearbook were brought up-to-date by the staff of the Directorate for Social Affairs, Manpower, and Education.

1970	7·2 per cent	1960–70	+2·0
1974	7·1 ,, ,,	1970–74	−0·1

We note that expenditures as a percentage of the GNP more than doubled from 1950 to 1970, from 3·0 to 7·2. The expansion from 1950 to 1960 is mainly accounted for by the large age groups born in the early 1940s. The age cohorts began to decrease in 1944, but the enrolment explosion in secondary education in the late 1950s and early 1960s, together with the major reforms of primary and secondary schooling, resulted in rising costs. The number of university students quadrupled from 1955 to 1968 and the costs for undergraduate education grew rapidly due to legislation passed in the 1950s on automatic staff allocation according to size of enrolment in the various university departments.

TABLE 5

Enrolment Rates by Year for Students in the Age Groups 15–18 and 20–24

Country	Year	15–18-year-old students	Rank order	Year	20–24-year-old students	Rank order
Austria	1969	31·9	14	1972	14·8	12
Belgium	1966	54·2	7	1971	20·5	6
Canada	1970	78·1	2	1970	28·8	2
Denmark	1970	51·7	9	1972	23·7	3
Finland	1967	47·4	10	1972	13·8	13
France	1970	54·3	6	1972	17·0	10
Germany	1969	30·5	16	1972	17·1	9
Ireland	1971	47·0	11	1970	12·2	14
Italy	1966	30·8	15	1972	20·1	7
Luxembourg	1970	37·4	13	1972	1·9	16
Netherlands	1970	52·5	8	1971	21·2	5
Norway	1970	68·9	3	1972	19·0	8
Sweden	1972	68·1	4	1972	22·4	4
Switzerland	1970	62·6	5	1972	10·3	15
United Kingdom	1970	39·4	12	1972	15·0	10
United States	1970	82·9	1	1972	51·5	1

Sources: Enrolment rates for 15–18-year-olds were adapted from UNESCO (1974, Tables 15 and 16, pp. 28–9); enrolment rates for 20–24-year-olds were adapted from UNESCO (1975, Table 3·2).

During the 1960s, as reported in conjunction with the

OECD conference on educational policies and economic growth in 1970 (OECD, 1971b), the educational expenditures in the member countries increased twice as rapidly as the GNP. The annual increase of expenditures (at current prices) was on the average 14 per cent between 1960 and 1970 (OECD, 1977b).

Thus the enrolment explosion at the secondary level has, as we have seen, been triggered by increased birth and participation rates. Behind the latter has been the 'revolution of rising expectations' which is a result of both economic growth and structural changes which opened secondary and higher education to new groups in society.

Education is a highly labour-intensive enterprise. The staff costs amount to some 75–85 per cent of the total expenditures in the industrialized countries. The unit costs could therefore be expected to rise more rapidly than the consumer price index, because the staff salaries in teaching at least during the 1960s tended to rise at a higher rate than the cost of living.

As long as the growth of expenditures could be accommodated within the margin provided by an expanding economy, be legitimated by public commitment to education, and enlist political support, the spectacular priority given to education was accepted. But when the economic leeway diminished and expanded educational provisions had to be carried by increased taxes, the 'headlong retreat' in commitment to education began at the end of the 1960s and early 1970s. Assessment of benefits began to be replaced by assessments of costs. Demands for accountability became vociferous. Budget-cutting and cost-conscious politicians began to air misgivings about what the educational system was 'producing'.

Cost development is likely to be intensely watched in the years to come considering the prospects for economic growth—or non-growth. It is within the realities of economic stagnation (or even decline), political instability, and a climate of frustration in the school that resource allocation decisions are likely to be made in the next ten years. After a period of boundless expansion and generosity with public resources those who represent education will, in Kenneth Boulding's (1975) words, have to adapt themselves to a 'management of decline'.

A CASE STUDY OF COST DEVELOPMENT:
THE CITY OF STOCKHOLM*

I have noted that the heavy increases in educational expenditures in the industrialized countries have been affected by changes in organizational structure and curriculum as well as by changes in fertility and participation rates. Rather little has been done to elucidate the development of the unit cost, the student cost per year. To conduct such studies will require access to itemized information about operational and capital expenditures. But access to such information at the national level (which unfortunately is seldom available) does not suffice. We also need qualitative indices, such as achievement test scores, which can give us information about the outcomes of the educative efforts made in the school. The information we have is usually, however, limited to quantitative indices that pertain to enrolment, dropout, and graduation rates. This is a pure 'head count' and does not give us any information about the quality of the products the school is turning out. Availability of qualitative measures of outcomes is exceptional both at the national and local level. The international surveys conducted by the International Association for the Evaluation of Educational Achievement (IEA) in 20 countries and the National Assessment are the main exceptions to this (Walker, 1976; Passow *et al.*, 1976).

At the local level itemization of expenditures is occasionally differentiated enough to allow greater in-depth analysis than at the national level. Such is the case with data from the Board of Education of the City of Stockholm. The Board issues each year a report with an itemization that allows a differentiated study of cost development.

The data at our disposal on school expenditures in the City of Stockholm ran from 1948 to 1975. For various reasons, particularly since the change in school structure affected comparability, we decided to limit the analyses to the period 1963–75. Two types of unit cost were studied: costs per student per year, and per student per period of instruction ('instructional hour'). In order to establish comparability between the thirteen

* The study briefly summarized here was conducted specially for the Aspen project. It will be reported in more detail by Jeffrey Bulcock.

fiscal years in the study we had to control for inflation and for changes in enrolment. The control for inflation was done by transforming the financial data into constant prices. The educational expenditures for a given year were adjusted by means of a price index which allowed an estimate of changes over time in expenditures in real terms. Control for enrolment changes was made by limiting the analyses to the mandatory school age, that is to say the age range 7 to 16, which is covered by the nine-year comprehensive school legislated for the entire country in 1962. More important, all cost data were calculated on a per student basis, either per student and year or per student and instructional hour.

The school reform entailed a considerable broadening of educational objectives. The implementation of this meant curricular provisions which implied the construction of facilities and expanded specialized provisions for teaching, for example, vocational subjects. The custodial standards were raised with resulting increases in operational and capital costs for provision of sport facilities, skating rinks, cafeterias, and health rooms. Operational costs include salaries for custodial, kitchen, and health personnel, and the recurrent provision of equipment.

Special and compensatory education were considerably expanded. According to regulations issued in the early 1960s, up to 15 per cent of the children could be assigned to special education arrangements with subsidies from the government. Since the classes for the mentally handicapped or clinics for those with emotional disturbances and reading disabilities are taken care of by teachers with additional training and higher salaries, and since the special classes are much smaller than the regular ones, the per student costs in special education are very high. Another expenditure of importance in the efforts to provide compensatory education for the disadvantaged are the programmes for the immigrant children whose mother tongue is not Swedish. Recent legislation has made provisions for these children with two hours of instruction per week in their mother tongue. Teachers in charge of this, often from the home country of the parents, also act as teacher aids in the regular classroom, thereby easing the transition to Swedish.

We first studied the changes in per student expenditures per year over the period 1963–75. As can be seen from Table 6 and

TABLE 6

Changes in Student Expenditure Per Instructional Hour in the City of Stockholm Comprehensive Schools 1963–1975 (Skr)

Year	Per student expenditure at current prices	Per student expenditure in constant prices (1968 = 100)	Per student expenditure per instructional hr. current prices	Per student expenditure per instructional hr. constant prices	Annual percentage increase in expenditure per hour
1963	2,472	3,793	2·29	3·51	—
1964	2,711	3,874	2·51	3·59	2·28
1965	3,091	3,981	2·86	3·69	2·78
1966	3,465	4,034	3·21	3·73	1·08
1967	4,082	4,278	3·78	3·96	6·17
1968	4,447	4,447	4·12	4·12	4·04
1969	5,123	4,902	4·74	4·54	10·19
1970	5,855	5,195	5·42	4·81	5·95
1971	6,469	5,117	5·99	4·74	—1·45
1972	7,538	5,539	6·98	5·13	8·23
1973	8,374	5,678	7·75	5·26	2·53
1974	9,665	5,813	8·95	5·38	2·28
1975	11,439	5,904	10·59	5·47	1·67

Source: Annual Reports of the Board of Education of the City of Stockholm. Based on a six-hour school day, 180-day school year, cf. Passow *et al.* (1976, p. 262).

Figure 4, the current prices have risen exponentially from Skr 2,472 in 1963 to Skr 11,439 in 1975. A similar rise has taken place in terms of student cost per instructional hour, from 2·29 to 10·59. In order to establish comparability in real terms we have adjusted the prices to the 1968 level (1968 = 100). We then find that in terms of the 1968 prices the per instructional hour cost has risen from Skr 3·51 in 1963 to Skr 5·47 in 1975. Thus in *constant* prices the cost for one instructional hour has over the twelve-year period increased by 56 per cent. It should be noted that the average annual increase of 3·8 per cent in constant prices is somewhat higher than the average increase in GNP over approximately the same peroid (3·1 per cent in 1965–73). Thus, the share of the nation's resources being allocated to public education—at least in Stockholm—has well kept pace with the real growth of national income.

In Figure 4 the cost development figures given in Table 6 are

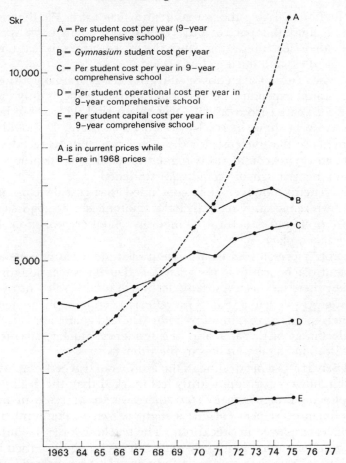

Skr

A = Per student cost per year (9–year
    comprehensive school)

B = *Gymnasium* student cost per year

C = Per student cost per year in 9–year
    comprehensive school

D = Per student operational cost per year in
    9–year comprehensive school

E = Per student capital cost per year in
    9–year comprehensive school

A is in current prices while
B–E are in 1968 prices

Fig. 4 Compulsory Schooling Expenditures per Student for the City of
Stockholm 1963–75.

Source: Annual Reports of the Board of Education of the City of Stockholm
1963–75.

graphically presented. But in addition the expenditures (in
constant prices) have to some extent been broken down. The
purpose has been to identify certain specific items that might
account for increases in expenditures. But the breakdown has
been difficult to accomplish, since in 1970 the budgetary procedures underwent revision which somewhat affected the

method of analysing the per student expenditure. We therefore had to limit this part of our comparisons to 1970–75 which made them less interesting, since the expenditures in real terms ceased to expand during that period.

We have also broken down educational costs into operational and capital expenditures. We could in these respects only compare the years 1970 to 1975. Over this period the costs in both these respects have in 1968 prices been constant. It should be pointed out that the costs for the *gymnasium* students (grades 10 through 12) are considerably higher than those for the nine-year comprehensive school (*grundskola*) students.

In general, however, it is concluded that cost development has been remarkably regular and monotonic since 1963 in spite of the profound structural changes in school organization that have taken place.

Table 7 presents an examination of student enrolments and student/teacher ratios in the *grundskola*. During the period under review there has been a steady decline of total enrolment by an average 3½ per cent a year. This reflects a common phenomenon in metropolitan areas in many industrialized countries. It is due to declining birth rates and the tendency among parents of child-producing age to live in the suburbs.

There is also a net decline in the number of teachers employed which, however, is significantly less marked than the decline in enrolment. From 1963 to 1971 there was a decrease in total enrolment of 21 per cent but a slight *increase* in the number of teachers employed in Stockholm. The teaching force (including the administrators) has, however, been declining since then but at a slower rate than student enrolment. This is reflected in the student/teacher ratio which has been going down, from 18 in 1963 to slightly above 13 in 1975.

Finally, we have also examined the relationship between teacher/student ratios and per student costs. To what extent are increasing expenditures a function of declining student/teacher ratios? We found that student/teacher ratios over time were highly correlated with per student costs (in constant prices) and accounted for as much as 78 per cent of the variation in costs between the fiscal years. With all the reservations that should be attached to the method used, there is evidence in support of the proposition that the cost increase per student of 56 per cent

TABLE 7

Student Enrolments and Student/Teacher Ratios in the City of Stockholm Comprehensive School System 1963–1975

	Number of students in comprehensive schools	Annual percentage decline in student enrolment	Number of teachers	Number of administrators	Total teachers and administrators	Annual percentage change in teacher and administrative appointments	Student/teacher ratio 1 (teachers only)	Student/teacher ratio 2 (teachers and administrators)
1963	80,866	—	4,514	282	4,796	—	17·91	16·86
1964	78,494	2·93	4,410	284	4,694	−2·13	17·80	16·72
1965	76,485	2·56	4,245	295	4,540	−3·28	18·02	16·85
1966	74,363	2·77	4,257	296	4,553	−0·29	17·47	16·33
1967	71,774	3·48	4,970	297	5,267	+15·68	14·44	13·63
1968	70,465	1·82	4,849	305	5,154	−2·14	14·53	13·67
1969	67,885	3·66	4,724	297	5,021	−2·58	14·37	13·52
1970	65,686	(4.680)*	292	4,972	−0·98	14·03	13·21
1971	63,817	3·24	4,637	292	4,929	−0·86	13·76	13·00
1972	60,424	2·84	4,347	302	4,649	−5·68	13·90	12·95
1973	57,739	5·32	4,145	296	4,441	−4·47	13·93	13·00
1974	55,124	4·44	3,965	297	4,262	−4·03	13·90	12·93
1975	52,818	4·53	3,971	293	4,264	±0·00	13·30	12·39

Source: Stockholm Office of Statistics, Statistical Yearbooks 1969, 1973, 1974, 1975.
* Estimate.

in constant prices over the period studied is due to a large extent to the lowering of the student/teacher ratio.

The enrolment explosion in the highly industrialized countries since the Second World War has been a snowball effect of high economic growth, high birth rate, increased social demand for education, and political choices by governments. But in addition to the increased number of participants in formal education there has been, as demonstrated by the case study of Stockholm, a considerable increase in unit cost. This latter increase is a source of serious concern at a time of minimal or zero growth in the economy.

The overwhelming portion (80 per cent as compared to 60 per cent in other sectors) of operational expenditures in education is staff salaries. Since these salaries all over the world tend to outpace the rise in general cost level, the unit cost is bound to go up unless certain rather radical steps in staff utilization are taken.

It is, needless to say, extremely difficult to project future enrolment and ensuing cost development. We have seen how, for instance, demographic changes can take forecasters by surprise. It is even more difficult to project the future social demand for education.

In order to manage within the existing financial resources cost cuts have to be achieved by better use of staff resources and by avoiding waste of time, including teaching time. A reduction of contact hours between teachers and students can mean considerable savings.

I agree with the OECD expert committee (OECD, 1977b) that, given the present social demand for education, it would be 'unrealistic' to expect a reduction of educational costs in the near future. On the basis of analysis of present cost trends and attempts to predict future enrolment, the group estimates that until 1985 educational expenditures will increase by between one-half and one per cent of the GDP, which, however, given the present growth rate of the resources, I seriously doubt.

5

Education and Equality

THE role of education in shaping a just and more equal society has been conceived quite differently depending upon the underlying social philosophy of the educators. For example, functionalists, such as Bell (1973) and Inkeles (1974), view education as a rational means of selecting and preparing people according to their abilities for the various positions in a complex, hierarchically organized society. On the other hand, neo-Marxists, such as Bourdieu (1964) and Carnoy (1974), conceive schooling in modern industrial society as a means of preparing docile and disciplined workers. The school is geared to reproduce the prevailing class differences.

The functionalist view is closely related to the classical liberal view that social mobility will be promoted by equal opportunity in access to education. The roots of the classical liberal conception of equality of educational opportunity are to be found in the eighteenth century with Locke, Helvetius, and, most influential of all, Jean Jacques Rousseau. In *Le Contrat Social* of 1762 he spells out how in the 'natural' state men are born equal, and how their rights are determined within the framework of the 'general will'. There are innate differences in personal qualities but these do not jeopardize social equality as long as society rewards people according to their merits and not according to birth and wealth. A 'natural aristocracy' emerges in a society that dissolves the privileges that form a basis for 'artificial aristocracy', an expression that means the same as 'ascriptive' aristocracy in modern sociology.

The famous Preamble of the American Declaration of

Independence of 1776 was first drafted by Thomas Jefferson who was influenced by Helvetius and Rousseau. When he and the other Founding Fathers said that 'all men are created equal' they meant that all are born with the same moral and political rights, not that they are endowed with equal capacities and qualifications. When Jefferson used the expression 'natural aristocracy' he meant the same as Rousseau, namely that no artificial barriers should prevent individuals from achieving the social statuses that match their talents.

The 'father of the common school', Horace Mann, by the mid-nineteenth century secretary to the School Board of the state of Massachusetts, belonged to the same tradition. He saw the school as an instrument of the open society for obtaining social justice, eliminating poverty, and achieving equality of opportunity. Often quoted as labelling the school as the 'Great Equalizer', he considered the common public school to hold the promise of providing equality of opportunity and of shaping a society free of social and economic inequities. Every person should be given an equal opportunity to achieve and to be promoted, provided he had the talent and the energy to get ahead. The school that selects and prepares young people for the different positions in society was assumed to perform these functions in a spirit of equity and impartiality. Its selective function was assumed to occur strictly according to proven merits and not to social background, sex, or race. The big individual differences in income, wealth, and power that after all are highly conspicuous in a society that has realized the meritocratic principles, are largely accounted for by innate differences in ability to get ahead in life. Thus in *one* sense a meritocratic society is 'classless', because in principle it offers every person an equal opportunity to become prosperous and influential.

Similar strains of thought are to be found among many of the European liberals who fought for a common basic school that would put young people on an equal footing in realizing their different talents. Equality of opportunity was by many implicitly conceived in terms of social Darwinism: 'Everyone in the jungle (or in society, or in school) was to be treated equally: one standard, one set of books, one fiscal formula for children everywhere, regardless of race, creed and color. Success went to the resourceful, the ambitious, the bright, the strong. Those who failed were stupid or shiftless, but whatever the reason, failure was the responsibility of the individual (or perhaps of his parents, poor fellow) but certainly not that of the school or the society.' (Schrag, 1970, p. 70)

The rethinking about the equality problem that has been going on in recent years has widened the perspective on the consequences of social Darwinism. The question has been raised whether one should not also consider what comes out of the system, that is to say whether equality of *results* is more important than equality of initial opportunity. The practical implication of this is that extra resources should be provided for those who are socially and culturally disadvantaged. This has, for instance, been the philosophy behind what in the 1960s emerged as programmes of 'compensatory education', most well known of which was the Headstart Program. In the 1966 report to the United States Office of Education (Coleman *et al.*, 1966) it is pointed out that 'equality of educational opportunity implies not only "equal" schools but equally effective schools, whose influence will overcome the differences in the starting point of children from different social groups'. (p. 72) The implication in terms of policy that ensues from the rethinking of the concept of equal opportunity is that it is rather pointless to put the final responsibility for scholastic success or failure on the individual. One has to shift the burden of responsibility to the system—to the educational system and/or to society at large.

The liberal vision of equal opportunity prevailed in most Western industrial countries until the late 1960s. The educational systems were part of a process of spectacular economic growth and expansion. The rising standard of living stimulated the social demand for education. The conception of education as a capital investment with high rate of return both to the individual and to society justified that the education sector in the late 1950s and during the 1960s was allowed to grow at a higher rate than the economy at large. By removing economic barriers and making more places available in upper secondary and higher education and by increasing the length of attendance in the common school, ideal conditions could be created to implement the vision of equal opportunity, where everybody had access to the kind and amount of education that suited his inherited capacity.

The late 1960s, not least the upheaval of 1968, marked a turning point. The power of the formal school system to serve as an equalizer was brought into question by participation studies conducted during the 1960s in the OECD countries (OECD, 1971a). Furthermore, the assumption that greater equalization of educational opportunities would in its wake have enhanced equalization of life chances turned out to be less valid than the optimists had anticipated. In his keynote address to the OECD Conference in 1970 on Policies for Educational Growth the Swedish Minister of Education had the following to say about education as a promoter of social change:

It is possible that we have been too optimistic, particularly perhaps concerning the time it takes to bring about changes. On the other hand, it is hardly possible to change society only through education. To equalize educational opportunities without influencing working conditions, the setting of wage rates, etc. in other ways, would easily become an empty gesture. The reforms in educational policy must go together with reforms in other fields: labour market policy, economic policy, social policy, fiscal policy, etc. (OECD, 1971b, p. 69).

Referring to the optimistic statements made during the first OECD Policy Conference on Education in Washington, D.C. in 1961, Charles Frankel and A. H. Halsey in their summary report (OECD, 1971b) from the 1970 Conference conclude:

Too much has been claimed for the power of educational systems as instruments for wholesale reform of societies which are characteristically hierarchical in their distribution of chances in life as between races, classes, the sexes and as between metropolitan/ suburban and provincial/rural populations. The typical history of educational expansion in the 1950s and the 1960s for the OECD countries can be represented by a graph of inequality between the above-mentioned social categories which has shifted markedly upwards without changing its slope. In other words, relative chances have not altered materially despite expansion. (p. 14)

In his Preface to Husén (1975) the Director of CERI (Centre for Educational Research and Innovation), James R. Gass, points out that policies that derive from the notion of making access opportunities formally equal have proven to have a 'disappointingly limited impact'. The reappraisal inspired by the partial failure of previous policies would have to consider measures that go beyond the removal of entrance 'obstacles to positive political measures of compensations and support, with the ultimate aim of a more equal social outcome'. (p. 3)

The whole issue of equalization of life chances and educational opportunities in particular was still rather unsophisticated in the early 1960s, which explains why it was viewed as a matter of simply removing social, economic, and geographical obstacles to access to furthergoing education. But a higher level of sophistication was achieved over the next decade owing to three circumstances.

(1) The fundamental problem of how individual differences in educability emerge and develop became the focus of an intensive debate and hence was further analysed and empirically studied.

(2) A series of important surveys of how differences in educational attainments were related to socio-cultural background were conducted, and their policy-orientation inspired a debate which brought up basic technical and theoretical problems (Coleman *et al.*, 1966; HMSO, 1967; Walker, 1976; and Jencks *et al.*, 1972). The studies by Jencks and his associates of the development of inequalities in life chances, and the IEA cross-cultural investigations of the relative importance of home and school in accounting for differences among students and schools in, for instance, reading and science, deserve mentioning here.

(3) The very concept of equality, for instance equality of opportunity versus equality of results, became the subject of philosophical analysis. Before the end of the 1960s Coleman (1968) was the only one among educational researchers who had attempted to clarify the concept. But after that a deeper and more faceted debate on equality emerged with contributions from Rawls (1971), Frankel (1973), and others.

In the following sections I shall expand these three aspects of the issue of equality in education. I shall also consider the related questions of, when should students of differing abilities be separated? To what degree does school make any difference to academic achievement? Finally, what is the role of the courts in implementing equality? Consideration of these issues will reveal the real dilemmas in achieving equality in education.

SCHOOLS, IQ, AND EQUALITY

On the surface, the problem of the relative importance of genetic and environmental factors in intellectual development —the nature–nurture dichotomy—might seem a rather esoteric academic issue. This does not mean that the problem has no policy implications. On the contrary, at the beginning of the testing movement it strongly influenced eugenic policy, for instance, legislation on sterilization of persons with low IQ, and on setting immigration quotas in the United States in the early 1920s. The vehement controversies in the wake of the famous Jensen (1969) article in the *Harvard Educational Review* indicate that we are here touching deeply rooted values underlying political ideologies. Levin (1972), in reviewing Jencks's (1972) controversial and explicitly policy-oriented book *Inequality*, has referred to this phenomenon as the 'social science objectivity gap'. The existence of such a 'gap' is evident to the reader of the extensive research literature on the heredity–environment issue. Statistically expressed findings are often interpreted quite differently as either supporting or refuting a hereditarian or an environmentalist interpretation of individual and group differences, depending upon the value orientation of the researcher.

The conservative, and usually meritocratic, conception of the issue is that human abilities are almost entirely inherited and that differences in educational attainment and life careers are largely accounted for by differences in cognitive abilities, and, to some extent, work motivation. A school system that does not take such inherited differences into account is 'fighting against nature'. Selective provisions have to be made to take care of the élite. Broadening of access to advanced education easily leads to an exhaustion of the resources of talent and to a lowering of standards.

Cyril Burt in England for a long time provided the scholarly ammunition to the hereditarians. His twin studies (1966) were regarded by Jensen (1969) as the most convincing evidence in support of the hereditarian view, until Kamin (1974) and others subjected the consistency of the statistical information to critical scrutiny. Burt represented the Galtonian tradition of 'hereditary genius'. Inspired by his interest in mental inheritance, Galton at the beginning of the century proposed to the British Association for the Advancement of Science that a survey on mental capacities be conducted. Together with Spearman, another pioneer in the intelligence test movement in England, Burt was assigned to develop the tests that were used in large-scale surveys (Husén, 1974b).

On the basis of his hereditarian view Burt (1972) sided with the *Black Papers*, two pamphlets published by a right-wing group in the British Conservative Party (Cox and Dyson (eds.), 1969 and 1970), against those who were proponents of a comprehensive secondary school and who wanted to abolish the eleven-plus examinations.

Another psychologist, Richard Herrnstein (1971 and 1973) of Harvard, first in an article in the *Atlantic Monthly* under the seemingly innocuous title 'IQ' and then in a book with the more explicit title *IQ in the Meritocracy*, spelled out the social implications of the genetic foundation of IQ. The implications are again meritocratic and are summarized in the Preface of his 1973 book:

There is evidence not only for the genetic ingredients in mental capacity but also in social status. Many of the means and ends of contemporary social policy fail to take into account those biological constraints, and they may consequently misfire. Equalizing educational opportunity may have the unexpected and unwelcome effect of emphasizing the inborn intellectual differences between people. It may instead be better to diversify education . . . Even the effort to encourage social mobility may have its penalties. The biological gap between social classes will grow if the people who rise from lower to higher status are selected for their native ability. (p. 10)

The conclusion is that a radical policy of egalitarianism would exhaust the amount of talent in the lower class, widen the 'ability gap' between social strata, and create a caste system wherein there would be little or no traffic across class boundaries. 'By removing arbitrary barriers between classes, society achieves the laudable goal of allowing people of different races, religions, and ethnic backgrounds to earn any level of status, but, simultaneously, it fosters biological barriers to mobility. When people can freely take their natural level in society, the upper class will, virtually by definition, have greater capacity than the lower.' (Herrnstein, 1973, p. 221)

The logic behind Herrnstein's reasoning can be summarized as follows:

(1) There is an objective set of psychological traits which constitute 'intelligence' (IQ);

(2) Individual and group differences in IQ have a large genetic component;

(3) IQ is of strategic importance for many high-level positions in society of today; and

(4) Therefore, IQ differences account for a considerable part of differences in social status and life success.

The key problem here is: on the basis of what values are criteria of stratification arrived at? It is my contention that the issue whether upper-class students are more 'intelligent' than lower-class students is a pseudo-problem, 'because the answer could logically be derived from the way the problem is posed'. The tests employed to measure intelligence have been validated against criteria of success in present society, such as school attainments and occupational status. These criteria reflect certain dominant values in our society. 'If we keep in mind that intelligence is defined by the dominant socio-cultural reference system, and that in the value structure guiding the system overriding priority has been attached to the ability to succeed in scholarly pursuits, one should not be surprised to find that upper-class students have higher IQ's than lower-class students and Whites perform better than Blacks.' (Husén, 1972, pp. 55-6) In other words, with intelligence defined within the framework of a meritocratic conception, the methodology employed will by necessity yield the results one expects.

HOW DIFFERENCES IN EDUCATIONAL ATTAINMENTS ARISE: NATURE VERSUS NURTURE

In a presidential address to the American Psychological Association Anne Anastasi (1958) pointed out that the task that lay ahead for research in the area of heredity–environment was to explore the *modus operandi* of genetic and environmental factors. They cannot, as had been assumed by most researchers in the field, be regarded as operating in an additive way. Instead they interact in a very complicated pattern which makes it extremely difficult to disentangle their respective 'effects'. Anastasi cites

Dobzhansky, a leading geneticist, who has advanced a striking illustration of how interaction can take place. Suppose that all persons with blood group AB are considered to be aristocrats while those with blood group O are considered inferior and only suited for menial labour; then blood group genes will in the course of time artificially become 'determiners' of certain types of behaviour. An example from the real world is the effect of discrimination against a particular social class or race. In the long run this will result in group differences which are correlated with genetic background without being causally affected by it.

Certain basic circumstances have seldom been considered in the debate. In the first place, there is no indication that cognitive behaviour of the type assessed by intelligence tests is monogenic. Secondly, endeavours to link genetic material, once identified with concrete cognitive behaviour, have not yet begun. Thirdly, the concept of 'heritability' which has played a key role in the debate does not apply to individuals but is, as pointed out by Dobzhansky (1973), a characteristic of a population. Estimates of heritability, if they are valid—which in itself is a doubtful proposition—are applicable only to the specific population studied by particular instruments at a particular point in time. It cannot be emphasized strongly enough that heredity is not a status but a *process*. The heredity component of a personality trait, say scholastic ability, can only be inferred from a process of development that is *not directly* accessible to observation and/or measurement. Fourthly, the method employed by Burt, Jensen, and others, who contend that the larger portion of individual differences is attributed to genetic factors, applies only to *individual* differences which are studied by means of identical twins, whereas policy makers are primarily interested in *group* differences which are more readily manipulated by policy measures.

The polarization that occurred in the scholarly world with regard to the heredity–environment issue in the early 1970s could hardly have been predicted by the late 1950s. But a decade later the political development had added new dimensions of applicability to a field of research that previously had been regarded as rather aloof and 'pure'. Studies of the relative importance of heredity and environment were supposed to provide answers to problems such as, 'Is compensatory education worthwhile?' or 'Do ghetto children fail because of innate inadequacies or because of social handicaps?' The overriding problem was the extent to which the educational system could rectify social handicaps in lower-class children or among racial minorities.

Prior to the Jensen debate many social scientists had shown an almost euphoric optimism about the possibilities of a system of advanced mass education, an optimism that became only slightly affected by the criticism and the vociferous quest for excellence in the wake of the Sputnik shock in the late 1950s. Robert Faris (1961) in a presidential address to the American Sociological Association was a spokesman for this optimism. It does not suffice, he said, to have a 'limited stock of geniuses at the top of the productivity organization'. (p. 836) By improving society one can also improve the conditions which promote the development of abilities. He further noted that 'a society generates its level of ability, the upper limit of which is unknown and distant', and best of all, the process of achieving that level is potentially subject to intentional control. The 'boom' in formal schooling could be seen as a 'potent instrument for raising the ability level of the population'. The nation was in his view at present 'quietly lifting itself by the bootstraps to an important higher level of general ability'. (p. 838)

Dobzhansky (1973) has attempted to bridge the gap between social philosophy and biology by bringing out the policy implications with regard to the heredity–environment issue. He underlines that equality should not be confused with identity. Equality is a social and not a biological concept.

Equality between various social, racial, and ethnic groups has often been confused with equal representation. Over the last few decades extensive survey research has consistently found tremendous differences between the upper and lower social classes in the portion of the relevant age group that has gone to upper secondary school and university. Such imbalances provide ample justification for hypothesizing that a large portion of the talented youth of lower-class background has not had the opportunity to enter further education and thus constitute an 'ability reserve'. But one cannot therefore jump to the conclusion that any imbalance, however small it may be, is entirely due to inequality of opportunity. The model of representational equality among social classes implies that cognitive characteristics are entirely determined by home background and that genetically determined intelligence is randomly distributed over social strata. We still have to account for the 'residual' factors. Only about half the variance in scholastic attainment has consistently been shown to be a result of home background, including such factors as parental education, verbal stimulation, and motivational support. Individuals vary not only in their actual intellectual capacity but also in their ability to take advantage of opportunities offered to them. There is ample evidence to show that both these capacities are also genetically affected.

Equality in education has two aspects. It is usually conceived in terms of social Darwinism: as the right to compete on equal terms with everybody else for access through the formal educational system to the various social positions. Equality could also be seen as the right to be treated differently according to one's particular abilities and interests. Different inherited capacities require different environments if they are to develop to the satisfaction of the individual. Equality of opportunity does therefore *not* mean identity of treatment.

The task of the educator is to bring about changes in the behaviour of growing or grown-up individuals. Such changes are achieved by environmental and not by genetic means and are accessible to direct observation. Since, as pointed out above, no links between specific genes and cognitive behaviour have been identified, the burden of proof as to how genetic factors act as restraints to educative efforts rests with the hereditarians and not with the environmentalists. Environmental influences on mental development are the only ones that can be directly observed and measured with the increasingly refined techniques developed within the behavioural sciences. What remains unexplained after the environmental influences have been assigned their 'share' could conditionally be referred to as genetic factors.

WHEN SHOULD STUDENTS OF DIFFERING ABILITY BE SEPARATED?

The core issue in British and Western European education at large over the last twenty-five years has been how early a separation of academically gifted from their peers should take place. Furthermore, in what type of institutions, selective or comprehensive in enrolment and programmes, should students of secondary school age be accommodated?* The main argument in favour of selecting students early and putting them into separate institutions has been that such a system caters better for able students and on the whole is conducive to the preservations of standards at all levels of ability. The main argument in favour of the comprehensive system has been one of social justice and equity, since it is expected to enhance educational opportunities for students from lower social strata.

Elitist and selective structures of secondary education have been supported by conservatives and traditional liberals, whereas those with left-liberal, social democratic, or 'socialist' views have favoured the comprehensive model. The British Labour Party has since the early 1950s favoured comprehensive secondary education; the Conservative Party has opposed it. A similar political constellation could at least until the beginning of the 1970s be noticed in the Federal Republic of Germany and in France.

The right-wing conservatives behind the *Black Papers* in England attacked the proposed or implemented reforms in British education, particularly the attempts to abolish streaming and the eleven-plus examinations and to introduce comprehensive secondary education. The 1944 Education Act had made provisions for universal secondary education within the framework of a tripartite school consisting of grammar schools, technical or vocational schools, and schools for the remainder, called 'secondary modern' schools. The first two were selective. The decisive point in the educational career of a student was the eleven-plus examination which decided not only who should be selected for grammar-school education but also in the long run who was eligible for higher education. There was a keen awareness among the parents of the fatefulness of the system and of its social class implications. Therefore, the Labour Party in certain districts began to implement a system of comprehensive secondary schools with all three secondary

---

* There is an extensive research literature dealing with the effects, cognitive or non-cognitive, of various differentiation and grouping practices, see e.g. Husén (1962), Svensson (1962), Borg (1966), Yates (1966), Dahllöf (1971).

programmes under the same roof; this facilitated movement from one programme to another, even if students were often 'streamed' according to their academic ability.

The two *Black Papers* with the subtitles *Fight for Education* and *The Crisis in Education* (Cox and Dyson (eds.), 1969 and 1970) contended that recent changes had brought about a marked decline in educational standards and that this threat to the quality of education stems from the 'ideology of egalitarianism'. Angus Maude, in a paper (1969) entitled 'The Egalitarian Threat', drew a distinction between equality of educational opportunity and egalitarianism. The egalitarian philanthropist is letting his emotions carry him away. 'In the name of "fairness" and "social justice", sentimentality has gone far to weaken the essential toughness on which quality depends.' The egalitarian 'instinctively dislikes any process which enables some children to emerge markedly ahead of their fellows'. He therefore attempts to destroy the schools that are taking special care of the most talented students. 'All kinds of education are not, as the egalitarians pretend, of equal worth and importance, nor can anything but harm come of claiming equal status for all kinds of educational institutions.' Equality of opportunity is recognized as a worthy ideal which cannot, however, be achieved quickly if one wants to avoid 'damaging the total quality of our society'. (p. 7)

In the Introduction to *Black Paper Two* (1970), the editors quote Maude as saying that one can have either equality *or* equality of opportunity and that one cannot have them both. In fact, the attempts to bring about equality are inimical to the attempts to achieve equality of educational opportunity.

Also in *Black Paper Two*, Szamueli makes the case that a comprehensive system that treats every student equally in terms of formal availability of education creates even greater inequality than the British elitist system. The goal should be to provide every child with the best possible chance to develop his particular talents in an optimal way. 'This', he goes on to say, 'can be accomplished only by an unequal, differentiated educational system, which levels out the handicap created for the able pupil by the inadequacies of his family's social and economic position'. (p. 49) The English grammar school has provided 'countless gifted working-class children with the opportunity to break down the class barriers and achieve unrestricted scope for their talents'. (p. 50) In referring to socialist systems, such as the ones in the Soviet Union and Hungary, Szamueli contends that the attempts to create equality in education are conducive to the preservation of social and economic inequalities that exist outside the school. He presents some statistical evidence, gleaned from Soviet publications, that appears to show that in the Soviet Union considerable disparities exist between, on the one hand, children whose parents are manual workers and peasants and, on the other, children from homes of the intelligentsia.

In the letter of transmission to the members of Parliament, *Black Paper Two* points out 'a marked decline in standards'. Reference is made to reading surveys conducted by Cyril Burt for the London County Council during the First World War and 55 years later. Her Majesty's Staff Inspector for mathematics is quoted as saying that the 'new' mathematics has been a failure. Children at twelve-plus do not any longer understand their tables. The increased number of pupils taking their 'O' and 'A' level examinations is by no means a proof of improvement in secondary education. It simply signifies that 'more means worse'. The comprehensive school is identified as the main cause behind the process of deterioration.

DOES SCHOOL MAKE ANY DIFFERENCE?

Some 30–40 years ago hopes were high for what the school could do in what Counts (1932) called 'building a new social order'. After the First World War a reformist wave swept education in the industrialized world. The Progressive Education Association expected the school to assume increased responsibilities for the education of young people and for bringing about social reforms. Similar views were held by the politicians behind the main report of the Swedish 1946 School Commission, who recommended a radical reform of the compulsory school system in the direction of comprehensivization:

The main task of the school is to educate democratic human beings . . . Only by means of free education can the school lay the foundations for a development of society shaped by the insight and free will of its citizens . . . The school in a democratic society must . . . constitute a milieu for the free development of children. The individuality and the personal assets of the pupil ought not only to be considered and respected but should form the starting point for how instruction and education of the child are laid out. The work in the school ought to aim at promoting a free and harmonious development of all aspects of the personality of the pupil but should at the same time develop what is unique and special with him. (SOU, 1948, pp. 3 ff.)

It would seem useful at this point to consider the constraints on what the school can do and deal briefly with what Lawrence Cremin (1976) refers to as the 'ecology of education'. In the first place, education cannot be identified with formal schooling only, for non-formal education is occurring in the context of other educational institutions, such as the family and mass media, whose role and impact over a short period have changed considerably. The contribution of the family to the outcomes of formal schooling has been the focus of interest among researchers and policy makers on both sides of the Atlantic since the mid-1960s when the strategy of compensatory education was developed (Leichter, 1974).

Moreover, the school's role has relative to other institutions diminished. It does not any longer, as was the case in the pre-industrial or neo-industrial society, possess a monopoly on imparting certain cognitive competencies. It has to compete with other institutions, such as the mass media. Out-of-school learning has gained so much in importance that the former omnipotence of the school as a knowledge transmitter has been lost.

Survey research conducted since the mid-1960s has given rise to a debate about whether 'school makes any difference'. The Coleman (1966) survey on equality of educational opportunity was commissioned by the United States Congress in order to evaluate the programmes launched to provide better education for the handicapped and ethnic minorities. The survey conducted in England by the Plowden Commission (HMSO, 1967) on 11-year-olds aimed at disentangling the relative influences of school and home on school attainments. Jencks (1972) and his associates reanalysed data from other surveys in order to study the impact of IQ, home background, and formal education on adult income. They arrived at the conclusion that the school only marginally accounts for differences in adult earnings. Finally, the IEA survey which comprised some twenty countries with students at three levels, 10-year-olds, 14-year-olds, and 18-year-olds respectively, could be cited (Walker, 1976).

I shall not enter here upon a discussion of the highly intricate technical problems, not to mention the difficult interpretation problems, one encounters in studies of this kind. Suffice it to say that a large proportion of individual differences in educational attainments are consistently accounted for by non-scholastic factors. The amount of variance explained by such factors varies of course between subject areas. Thus, the overwhelming portion of the variance in reading is accounted for by home background, whereas in the case of performance in foreign languages only a small proportion is explained by background factors. This does not, however, justify the conclusion that the school 'does not make much difference'. Evidently, the 'laying off' of the school would have catastrophic consequences in a highly complex, technological society with its complicated interaction between the school, home, and other agencies within the global environment that constitutes the educational ccology. The more advanced the education of parents and the more developed their consciousness about the value of education, the greater the likelihood that their children will take advantage of school instruction.

THE ROLE OF THE COURTS IN IMPLEMENTING EQUALITY

The preoccupation with equality of educational provisions in the Western world since the early 1960s has brought the courts into the arena of educational policy-making. The classical illustration is the 1954 ruling of the United States Supreme Court that marked the beginning of the end of racial discrimination. Civil rights legislation further reinforced the role of the courts in implementing reforms. The more intense the competition for admission to higher education, the more likely it becomes that suits are filed with courts in order to safeguard constitutional rights and prerogatives. So far, rulings made by courts in the United States and the Federal Republic of Germany have had a strong impact on educational policy and

practice. In Germany the constitutional court in Karlsruhe has
made rulings that pertain to university admission. This has
sometimes brought policies set by legislative bodies into conflict
with those set by court rulings. Sometimes court rulings have
countered progressive school reforms, as in the case of the Land
of Hesse in Germany where an administrative court ruled that
every child had the right to a three-track system (*dreigliedrige
Schule*) at the lower secondary level. This, by implication, was
a ruling against the comprehensive school (*Gesamtschule*), which
had begun to replace the previous system of three tracks, reflecting the structure of an ascriptive society with its three distinct
social groups.

DILEMMAS IN ACHIEVING EQUALITY IN EDUCATION

As has become increasingly evident, the traditional mode of
conceiving equality in education and of framing policy to
achieve equality of opportunity is beset with certain dilemmas.

The first basic dilemma lies in the fact that the educational
system is there to impart competencies and therefore almost by
necessity creates differences. The school cannot at the same time
serve as an equalizer and as an instrument that establishes,
reinforces, and legitimizes distinctions. As long as there is only
one approved avenue to the 'mainstream of dignity' for which
some are selected according to one single, linear standard
(bright, average, stupid) which implies that some are destined
to fail, people are lured to aspire for something they are unable
to achieve. To paraphrase Orwell: those who from the outset
are more equal than others will take extra advantage. Therefore, the problem of achieving real equality of opportunity is
one of providing multiple options based on different values that
are not ranked along only one dimension. Therefore, we have
begun to realize that uniform educational provision is not *the*
solution to a more equal society. Differences in biological assets
call for pluralism and not for identity in treatment.

The second basic dilemma is the one between equality and
meritocracy. We submit that it has become more acute in the
technological complex society. It was first in a drastic way made
explicit by Michael Young in his satire *The Rise of the Meritocracy*
(1958). The egalitarian–meritocratic dilemma cuts across various

types of economies and social orders. It emerges with force-
fulness in all highly industrialized countries, be they capitalist
or socialist. In his study of the coming post-industrial society,
Bell (1973) foresees a growing meritocracy. The movement
toward the 'new centrality of *theoretical* knowledge, the primacy
of theory over empiricism, and the codification of knowledge into abstract systems of symbols that can be translated
into many different and varied circumstances' (pp. 343–4)
means that rationality and systematized knowledge rather than
property and political status become the basis of influence and
power. Bell sees the ascendance of technology, and increased
bureaucratic controls which increase the influence of professional and scientific élites, as salient features of the post-
industrial society.

The equality–meritocracy dilemma is not just one of increased
power of educated intelligence or of the highly educated becoming more prestigious, more influential, and better paid. There
is also a tendency for meritocratic prerogatives to be passed on
from one generation to the next. The liberal conception of
meritocracy assumes a high degree of inter-generational mobility in social status due to intra-familial variation in capacity.
It assumes in the long run a 'just reshuffling' among the social
classes according to inborn capacity. Those who are born into
privileged circumstances, but genetically are 'regressions' towards the mean, will also regress in social status, whereas those
of high genetic potential in lower classes will, provided the
necessary effort is expended, move to a higher status. But the
notion that the social classes will sort themselves out according
to inborn capacity between generations is not supported by
particularly convincing evidence. One finds in widely different
social orders that those who 'made it' to advanced positions (not
least by means of advanced education) tend to pass on their
privileges to the next generation. In a society where the inheritance of wealth is nil or close to nil, the best parents in privileged
positions can do is to try hard to support their children in getting access to furthergoing attractive education. This is what
happens in socialist countries with their new élites.

The passing on of achieved status from one generation to the
next is in the meritocratic society a substitute for the inherited
privileges in the ascriptive society. All industrial countries are

very far from the inter-generational 'reshuffling' of statuses
believed in by those who advocate systematic meritocracy based
on intellect and effort. The 'new intelligentsia' in countries
which have recently gained independence and/or have gone
through a rapid process of modernization spearheaded by the
new educated class has a vested interest in preserving the privileges that have often been won with much work and sacrifice.
Lipset (1972) concludes, after having reviewed the literature on
social mobility, that 'advanced Communist countries have not
been more successful in removing all barriers to upward social
mobility than the advanced Western countries . . . And despite
the efforts of many societies to ensure that educational resources
are equally available to all, everywhere lower-class children
seem unable to take full advantage of them.' (p. 106)

There is an intrinsic element of meritocracy in the social
fabric of advanced industrialization. It is connected with a
strong demand for expertise with advanced training in such
fields as administration, technology, science, and communication (in a wide sense, including teaching). The necessity during
the 'take-off' period to recruit a new intelligentsia makes the
social status system somewhat more fluid. Ascriptive status
determined by birth and social background is partly replaced
by achieved status for which education becomes increasingly
important. In societies with universal secondary education and
in transition to mass higher education, furthergoing education
gains in importance not primarily for acquiring particular job
competencies but for maintaining one's competitive power in
the world of work. The employment system expects the educational system to do the sifting and sorting which in its turn
makes the educational system more competitive. With job re-
cruitment increasingly being done on the basis of certificates
and degrees, the better educated have better chances of climbing the social ladder than the less educated or, at least, do not
run the same risk of slipping down. Questions of examinations
and grades have become increasingly controversial as a result of
this development.

The strength of the meritocratic element depends upon the
value attached to economic growth as a worthwhile goal and
how one sees its compatibility with subjective indicators of the
'quality of life'. Since economic growth so closely depends on

efficient utilization of modern technology and management techniques, a premium will be placed on competence that will guarantee successful incumbents an increasing number of key positions. The solution to the equality problem is therefore intimately tied to how one resolves the problem of economic growth.

6

Have 'Standards' Declined?

MISGIVINGS

CONCERN about declining standards tends to be aired when educational systems are changed, particularly when opportunities for further education are expanded. The criticism levelled against the high school in the United States in the early 1950s is a case in point. Critics gathered evidence supportive of lack of intellectual rigour and deteriorating basic skills. The critics of mass secondary education on both sides of the Atlantic have mostly been speaking for the universities which traditionally had been the recipients of the products of the secondary school and who still tended to conceive its role mainly as that of preparing for the university. As Trow (1962) pointed out, the high school in the United States had over a period of a few decades gone through a spectacular expansion in terms of both enrolment and programmes to cater for all young people at the relevant age level. But the notion of the academically-oriented secondary school preparing for higher education still prevailed among professors, who suddenly found that that type of school fell shockingly short of their expectations.

CAN 'STANDARDS' BE ASSESSED?

Both educators and laymen often use the word 'standard' in passing sweeping judgements on the quality of school education. 'Standard' is indeed an old cherished notion in the pedagogical folklore, to the extent that it is almost conceived as metaphysically anchored. No wonder, therefore, that any lowering of standards is regarded as a sacrilege. It is striking to note how, at least in Europe, steps taken to broaden the opportunities for secondary and higher education have been consistently met by the objection that they would 'lower standards'. The gloomy forebodings in a way turn out to be true, since one finds that as the proportion of an age group enrolled in the non-compulsory secondary school increases average performance declines. Thus, if enrolment increases from, say, twenty to fifty per cent of an age group, as happened recently in some European countries, the average attainments of the fifty per cent will fall below those of the more select twenty per cent.

'Standards' can be given a rational meaning in two respects. First, they relate to the educational objectives set for a specific type of school in accordance with its curriculum. These objectives are as a rule expressed in general words about cognitive goals that should be achieved, but they can partly be operationalized in terms of specific competencies or behaviours. Second, the extent to which a given school type lives up to its curricular objectives can be described in simple statistics, such as mean reading age.

'Standards' can be perceived as something *absolute*. The student must attain a certain level of competence to get his 'pass' and/or qualify for the next stage or grade. The student is judged by whether or not he has scraped past the absolute standard limit, not by his relative position on a scale of achievement. This approach in assessing student competence is, to use the technical term of test experts, 'criterion-referenced'. Criterion-referenced evaluation of standards applies particularly to relatively static educational systems with a long tradition, where the requirements that have to be fulfilled in order to pass the examinations take on the character of being, as I put it above, metaphysically given.

'Standard' can also be expressed in *relative* terms, i.e. by comparing the individual student or class of students with the distribution of achievements in the relevant population. In this case it is not a preconceived set of competencies that is used as standard but the actual attainments in the reference population. The term is used in this sense about the 'standard tests' in the three Rs administered in Swedish schools since the mid-1940s in order to establish between-school equivalence of marking.

STANDARDS OF TOP STUDENTS IN COMPREHENSIVE
AND ELITIST SYSTEMS

A minimum of articulation has been reached when standards arc rated by comparing achievements at the same grade level over time or between regions or countries. Average level of competence in, for instance, mathematics can be compared between the upper secondary school of today and that of some twenty-five years ago, or between *Abiturienten* in the Federal Republic of Germany and high school leavers in the United States. Two difficulties are, however, encountered in such an exercise. The standard is supposed to be gauged in relation to stated objectives. For instance, a comparison between the academic, selective secondary school of yesterday and the comprehensive one of today would have to take into account differences in terms of objectives which have changed in connection with broadening of enrolment and programmes.

But a second and more essential comparability problem presents itself: one cannot indiscriminately compare school populations which comprise highly different proportions of the relevant age groups. There is no point in comparing the standard achieved in mathematics among upper secondary school students in a system with practically universal upper secondary schooling with that in a system where a small select fraction of the relevant age group proceeds to that level. The achievement standard in, say, mathematics of high school seniors in the United States is far below that of their age-mates in England who sit for the GCE or of the *Oberprimaner* in the Federal Republic of Germany. The pointlessness of such a comparison stands out when we find that 75 per cent of the relevant age group in the United States is compared with only 15–25 per cent in England or Germany.

The reason for the passion that has often gone into the controversy about a comprehensive versus a selective school system at the secondary level is not because didactic principles or curriculum organization are at issue. At the heart of the matter are two opposing educational philosophies which reflect strong vested interests.

A comprehensive system provides publicly supported school education for all children of mandatory school age in a given catchment area. All programmes are offered under the same roof. Another essential feature of comprehensiveness is that no organizational differentiation or grouping practices are employed that decisively give direction to the educational careers the students.

A selective system employs organizational differentiation at an early stage in order to allocate children to different types of schools or sharply divided programmes. Furthermore, grouping practices are employed at an early stage with the aim of spotting students who are considered to be academically oriented. Apart from selective access and internal grouping, the system has a high attrition rate in terms of grade-repeating and drop-out.

In the debate on the relative merits and drawbacks of the two systems it has been maintained, on the one hand, that the most able students in a comprehensive system will suffer by having to be taught together with their slow-learning peers. This will impair their standard in comparison with students of equal intellectual potential in selective systems. The adherents of comprehensive education, on the other hand, maintain that the better students will not suffer as much in that system as do the great mass of less academically-oriented students in a selective system.

Those in favour of the elitist system maintain that a system of selection based on fair and uniformly employed criteria of excellence will automatically open the avenues to high-status occupations to everybody who 'deserves' it, that is to say possesses the necessary (mainly inherited) talent and energy. The comprehensivists counter by claiming that the selective system is beset with a greater social bias than the comprehensive, since at the upper secondary and higher education levels the proportion of lower-class students consistently tends to be lower in a selective than in a comprehensive system.

The two propositions spelled out here—the standard of the élite and inherent social bias—were tested on national systems of education in the first two large-scale surveys conducted by the International Association for the Evaluation of Educational Achievement (IEA) (Husén, 1967; Postlethwaite, 1967; Comber and Keeves, 1973; Husén *et al.*, 1973). Some twenty national systems of education were investigated and found to differ considerably with regard to the relative number of students at the pre-university level. In the mathematics study that number varied from 10 per cent of the relevant age group in some European countries to more than 70 per cent in the United States. In the science study the variation was of the same order of magnitude. One could in this connection talk about differences in retention rate or 'holding power' at the upper secondary level in various countries. The high school seniors consist of more than 75 per cent of the relevant group in the United States, those who complete *gymnasium* in Sweden (grades 11 and 12) of some 45–50 per cent, and the *Oberprimaner* (grade 13) in the Federal Republic of Germany of some 15 per cent. There is evidently no point in comparing average performances of school populations representing such large variations in the proportion of the relevant age groups. Comparisons would make sense only with equal proportions of the entire age cohorts.

Such comparisons, however, are conducted under the assumption that those who are *not* in school (and who in this case have not reached the pre-university stage) have not, either by previous schooling or by other learning opportunities, achieved the competence reached by the élite still in school. On the basis of studies of achievements both at the beginning and at the end of secondary school it was concluded that those who were not in school would not have fallen into the top category of achievers, say, the top 5–10 per cent.

Another objection has been that a comparison of equal proportions of the age groups is unfair to national systems with low retention rate and/or high selectivity. The validity of this objection can be questioned on purely logical grounds, because it is not consistent with the elitist conception of how the educational system works. For in countries where until a few decades ago only some 5–15 per cent of the entire age group was retained up to the pre-university grade, the proponents of the system maintained that it efficiently took care of most of the able students without being biased against any other category. Thus the argument that selective systems lose a considerable number of the more able students has no force.

In the mathematics study (Husén, 1967) two types of between-country comparisons were made. In the first, mean performances of all the students taking mathematics were compared for twelve countries. The proportion taking mathematics varied from 4–18 per cent of the total age group. Therefore, the mean performances of the top 4 per cent in all the countries were compared. As can be seen from Figure 5, countries with a high retention rate moved up considerably.

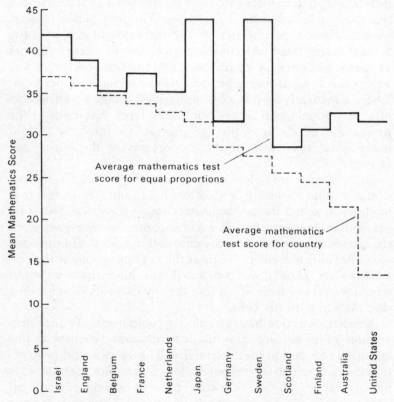

FIG. 5   Mean Mathematics Test Score (1) for the Total Sample and (2) for Equal Proportions of the Age Group in Each Country for Terminal Mathematics Populations.

Source: Husén (ed.) (1967, Vol. II, p. 124).

Analogous comparisons were conducted with terminal students in science (Husén *et al.*, 1973). It was decided to compare the top 9 per cent of the pre-university students in the industrialized countries. This percentage was chosen because it represented the lowest proportion of the age group at that level in any of the countries. In order to get measures for two more limited élites, the top 5 and 1 per cent were chosen. The outcomes of these comparisons are presented in Figure 6. If the means of the secondary school leavers, irrespective of their proportion within the relevant age group, are compared, we find that the United States is far behind all the other developed countries. When the top 9 per cent are compared, we find that countries with a high retention rate, such as the United States, get sharply increased mean scores. By and large, the same picture emerged when countries were compared with regard to the top 5 and 1 per cent of the age group.

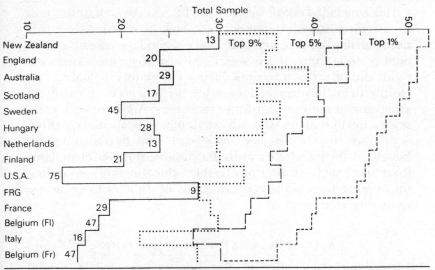

FIG. 6   Mean Science Scores for Total Samples of Pre-University Students and for the Top 9, 5, and 1 per cent respectively. For each country the size of the pre-university population as a percentage of the total relevant age group has been indicated.

Source: Husén *et al.* (1973, p. 146).

As pointed out above, in selective systems the high standard of the élite is often bought at the price of limiting the opportunities of the mass of the students (Husén, 1960). At the 14-year-old level practically the entire age group was in full-time schooling, whereas a varying proportion of the students had left school before the end of secondary school. By comparing the distributions of the status of parental occupations at the two levels an index of social selection can be derived. The proportion of fathers belonging to the professional and managerial category on the one hand and the semi-skilled or unskilled workers on the other were calculated. The index was unity when upper and lower strata had the same representation at the pre-university as at the 14-year-old level. The United States had an index of 1·3 and Sweden one of 2·4, both being countries with relatively retentive and comprehensive systems. The Federal Republic of Germany had an index of 37·7 and England of 7·9, both then being countries with more selective systems of education with early transfer from primary to academic secondary school.

It is concluded on the basis of the I EA surveys that the comprehensive system, by its openness, lack of selective examinations during the primary and lower secondary stages, and its high retention rate, is a more effective strategy for taking care of all the talent of a nation during mandatory schooling. By casting the net as widely as possible the prospects of 'catching' an optimum number of fish are increased. A system with early separation of students who are rated to have academic potential is destined to produce good *end products*. But this advantage is bought at the price of excluding a sizeable number of students from lower social strata from further education and of limiting the opportunities of the great majority of students to get access to quality education.

ASSESSING STANDARDS OVER TIME

In assessing the quality of education as mediated by formal schooling the ambition is to relate changes in standards to changes pertaining to learning conditions in a narrow sense, such as school resources, classroom practices, and teacher competence. Attempts to do so are made difficult by the problem that comparisons over time of student competence reflect not only changes in the learning conditions in the school environment *per se*, but also to a varying degree changes in non-scholastic conditions, such as characteristics of the population under consideration, particularly since the impact of socio-economic factors on achievement in certain subject areas is relatively strong. The Bullock Report (HMSO, 1975) points out: 'If [the] population alters between surveys, trends they identify will be partly, or even mainly, sociologically determined. It will thus be extremely difficult to isolate valid interpretations of changes of standards of reading, or for that matter of other cognitive abilities.' (p. 21)

In the IEA surveys of some twenty countries attempts were made by means of a multivariate technique to separate the total effects of learning conditions at school from the effects of the home environment (Peaker, 1975). Home background variables that were consistently related to the achievement variables were identified and formed a composite which was labelled 'school handicap score'. The variables selected were: father's occupation, father's education, mother's education, number of books at home, and size of family.

Two main types of analysis were employed to explain the variations in achievement in science, reading comprehension, and literature: between-school and between-student multiple regression analyses. (For details, see Peaker, 1975 and Walker, 1976.)

The explanatory variables were divided into four major 'blocks':

(1) Student background, consisting of School Handicap Score, age, and sex of the student;

(2) Type of school and type of programme within school;

(3) Learning conditions within the school;

(4) 'Kindred' variables, such as attitudes towards school and motivation for school work, which can be conceived of as input factors determining outcomes but also as outcomes of learning experiences.

The rationale for the analytic strategy used will not be discussed here. The methodological snags were by and large the same as those encountered in the Coleman *et al.* (1966) survey of equality of educational opportunity, and in the re-analyses of previous surveys by Jencks and his associates (1972).

Both Coleman (1975) and Härnqvist (1975) have collated the outcomes of all the analyses conducted in the IEA project in order to identify the salient explanatory factors in the domain of school learning and home background. The explanatory power of the various 'blocks' shows a remarkably consistent pattern over countries and age levels. In the between-school analyses 60–70 per cent of the variance is explained by the entire set of independent variables. Some 40 per cent is accounted for by background, whereas some 20 per cent by a combination of school type, school programme, and learning conditions in school. The rest is explained by 'kindred' variables.

In the between-student analyses only about one-third of the variance in achievement was explained by the whole set of independent variables. The following average percentages emerged from the between-student analyses:

	Science	Reading	Literature
Background	14	13	12
School type and programme	5	6	5
School learning conditions	11	6	5
Kindred factors	5	7	6
Total explained variance (per cent)	35	32	28

The relative explanatory power of the school factors was considerably larger in the IEA than in the Coleman (1966) or the Jencks (1972) surveys. However, the IEA study arrives at the same result as previous investigators, that is to say, that background factors tend to account for considerably more of the variation in achievement than factors constituting the learning conditions in the school itself.

In four of the six subject areas investigated by IEA home background accounted for more of the between-student variance in achievement than all the factors constituting the school learning conditions. Such findings have sometimes been interpreted to support the contention that 'school does not make any difference'. The between-school analyses produced, as pointed out above, much less potent measures of the influence of learning conditions than between-student analyses. Again, we must remember that it is a question of accounting for *variance*. Thus, the variation in educative 'effectiveness' between schools in general is narrow in comparison with the variation between homes. In a homogeneous country like Sweden the between-school variance amounts to about 10 per cent of the between-student variance, which indicates a great uniformity in school resources but also a remarkable homogeneity in student back-ground between catchment areas. In England and the United States the corresponding figure was over 20 per cent and in India it amounted to as much as 80 per cent. The average over all the IEA countries was about 25 per cent. Comparisons of student achievements over time are difficult to make because of changing patterns of objectives. Shift of emphasis occurs within and between subject areas, but the shifts can also affect the relative weight given to cognitive and non-cognitive objectives.

Two types of empirical evidence are available with regard to changes in cognitive standards: IQ scores and achievement scores over time. For a long time the question of whether IQ tended to decline from one generation to the next was a central issue in England—an issue referred to by Cattell as the 'fight for our national intelligence' (Cattell, 1937; Burt, 1946; Thomson, 1950). It was closely related to the issue of genetic conditions of intelligence and differential fertility. Surveys conducted in England and Scotland—in the latter region the entire age cohort of 11-year-olds was tested in 1932 and 1947—seemed to indicate that high-fertility families had children who on the average scored lower on intelligence tests than children from low-fertility families. Cyril Burt (1946) and others even tried to estimate the decline per generation that would result from this trend.

It would take us too far to spell out here the technicalities implied in studies of this type. They have been reviewed in detail elsewhere (see Husén, 1974b). Suffice it to point out that IQ surveys of representative populations compared over time consistently show that contrary to prediction the average IQ level tends to increase. This was the main finding in the Scottish mental surveys conducted in 1932, 1947, and 1956. It also applied to comparisons between United States draftees in 1917 and 1943 and Swedish conscripts from 1948 to 1953. The same trend is noted with regard to the standing height of the adult population in the same countries, which on the average is increasing in spite of the fact that there is a small negative correlation between number of children in the family and their height. It is concluded in Husén (1974b, p. 80): 'Considering our present knowledge a decline in mean intellectual performance is not in sight, on the contrary it seems to rise.'

EFFECT OF BROADENED ACCESS ON STANDARDS

It is often maintained that 'more means worse' when opportunities for further education are broadened. By admitting an increasing proportion of the age group one by necessity also lowers the standards among the entrants. Such a prediction is logically valid only under the assumption that in elitist systems, such as the ones at the secondary and post-secondary level in most European countries until recently, access to further education is granted only or mainly on the basis of proven competence and that social background plays an almost negligible role. There is abundant evidence that this assumption is false.

Policy actions taken to equalize opportunities for advanced education are purportedly based on promotion of ability (however defined) and on minimizing the influence of social background. Talent in all social strata should be given the same chance (by due assessment) to develop. According to the classical conception of equality of opportunity talent is chiefly genetically determined and therefore represents a strictly limited capital. Thus, once all possible actions have been taken to detect and develop ability above a certain IQ level, further broadening of opportunities would mean lowering of standards. The search for excellence has its own law of diminishing return.

Educators have for a long time been used to the idea that intellectual ability by some kind of inherent necessity is distributed according to the elegant, bell-shaped probability curve once advanced by Gauss. The majority of individuals is grouped in the middle around the mean, and there are increasingly fewer the more one moves towards the extreme. If this notion is associated with the one that ability is essentially inherited, the answer to the question of what would happen if, say, 25 instead of 5 or 15 per cent were enrolled in higher education is obvious: standards would go down. Before examining the proposition that an increase of enrolment beyond some 5 or 15 per cent of the age group lowers the standards, one should remember that scholastic aptitude is also constituted of non-cognitive attributes. Massive empirical evidence tells us that at most 50 per cent of individual differences in educational attainments are attributable to purely intellectual factors. The rest consists of motivation, interest, perseverance, health, and—not to forget—home background (Husén, 1975).

The bell-shaped distribution of IQ scores obtained when intelligence tests are administered to unsorted populations is by no means given in the nature of things or divinely ordained. It is simply an artifact of the 'norm-referenced' procedure by means of which the tests are constructed. As can be learned from any textbook on psychological and educational measurement, test exercises are chosen so as to cover symmetrically the entire range of difficulty. The latter is defined by the percentage of the population that is able to pass a given item. This procedure makes the distribution of said scores symmetrical and aesthetically so attractive. The size of the intercorrelations between items determines how slim or flat the curve will be.

With these technical observations in mind we can now examine some empirical evidence at hand on the effects on standards of broadening the enrolment in secondary and higher education. I shall briefly focus on two types of investigations: (1) surveys of the 'reserve of talent', and (2) studies of the effect on the distribution of intellectual ability when access to upper secondary and higher education is expanded.

(1) Surveys of the 'reserve of ability' (*Begabungs-reserve*) have been conducted in several countries, such as Sweden, the Federal Republic of Germany, Austria, France, and the United States. The primary aim of these studies has been to assess what percentage of an unsorted age group possesses the ability to profit from advanced formal education, and what percentage (in different social strata) has not had the opportunity or has not taken advantage of it, in spite of scoring above a certain level regarded as a prerequisite for such studies. The very expression 'reserve of ability' suggests that there is a genetically fixed pool of ability that has to be detected in order to become developed. The metaphor is therefore easily misleading. But there is evidence from longitudinal studies that the pool of talent *to some extent* is expandable. In the first place, we know that formal education *per se* can considerably improve IQ. The increment in IQ affected by the extra formal schooling from the age of 14 to 18–19 amounts to some 10–15 IQ points (Husén *et al.*, 1969). Furthermore, successive cross-sectional studies of complete age groups, such as the ones conducted on

11-year-olds by the Scottish Council for Educational Research, show improved average intellectual standards over time as measured by tests (Maxwell, 1961).

Back in the 1940s, when the first surveys in Sweden on the 'reserve of ability' were conducted with a rather crude methodology, I arrived at the somewhat conservative estimation that some 15 per cent of an age group was intellectually capable of passing the matriculation examination which was a prerequisite for university entry. Since by 1946-7, when these studies were published, only some 5-6 per cent of an age group actually sat for the examination, it appeared ridiculous to maintain that almost twice as many might belong to the 'reserve'. I dared in a 1951 article to maintain that the intellectual capital of a nation is not a fixed entity but is subject to the influences of social and economic policy which could not only better utilize this capital but expand it as well. By 1968, the year before the matriculation examination was abolished, some 20 per cent of the relevant age group passed the examination. Thus, the 'reserve' considerably exceeded the percentage that some twenty years earlier had been regarded as impossible.

(2) There is some evidence of the effect of increased enrolment on intellectual standards at the upper secondary and university levels. During the period 1918 to 1943 high school enrolment in the United States doubled, from 12 to 25 per cent of the relevant age group. Finch (1946) collected information on the distribution of intelligence test scores among high school students in a large number of studies from 1918 on. The mean scores for all these studies were plotted against the time axis. The ensuing curve, contrary to expectations, showed an upward trend. In addition, Finch compared the scores of two high school populations from the same area in the State of Illinois, the first tested in the early 1920s and the second some twenty years later. The area study also came out with an increase in mean score. Berdie (1962) and his associates have found the same trend in the State of Minnesota, where they studied the development of intellectual standards from 1928 to 1960.

In a study commissioned by the Carnegie Commission on Higher Education, Taubman and Wales (1972) collated information on the intellectual level of American college entrants from 1920 to 1965. They found that during that period the average level of ability among college entrants had risen from the 53rd to somewhere between the 60th and 65th percentile among an unsorted population of high school leavers. The difference between entrants and non-entrants increased considerably: from 5 percentile points in 1920 to 25–30 points in the 1960s. These findings tell us that intellectual capacity, as assessed by scholastic aptitude or I Q tests, plays a more important role in the United States now than some 40–50 years ago in determining entry to higher education. We do not have access to a record over the same length of time in Europe. There are, however, indications that the same trend applies to recent European developments in university enrolment. The relative size of the 'reserve of talent', despite remaining social imbalances, is likely to have diminished recently as a result of increased participation and the removal of geographical and economic barriers to furthergoing education. We can conclude from the evidence at hand that the increase of secondary school graduates entering university has been particularly intense in the top quartile of the scholastic aptitude distribution (Svensson, 1977).

CHANGES IN ACHIEVEMENT STANDARDS

The committee of inquiry into the teaching of reading and of other uses of English under the chairmanship of Lord Alan Bullock (H MSO, 1975) devoted one chapter to the assessment of standards in reading in England, since concern about literacy was the main reason why the Committee was appointed. Two sources of information about the standards in reading were used: (1) testimonies of expert witnesses, and (2) empirical surveys. Methodological difficulties encountered in making comparisons over time are pointed out. Accurate sampling procedures began to be employed in national surveys rather late. The validity of the tests employed changes over time: 'The problem . . . is one of attempting to assess the product of a variety of contemporary aims and methods with instruments constructed many years ago.' (p. 16) The general picture is one of rising reading scores through the 1950s and 1960s with a slight decline by 1970. It is concluded: 'At the age of 11 no significant change in reading standards over the decade 1960–1970 emerges from the N.S. 6 (reading test used in the national survey conducted by National Foundation for Educational Research) survey. The indicators are that there may now be a growing proportion of poor readers among the children of un-skilled and semi-skilled workers. Moreover, the national vari-ances almost certainly mask falling standards in areas with severe social and educational problems.' (p 25)

Findings that suggest a decline in the United States in achievement test scores, particularly in the widely used Scholastic Aptitude Test (SAT), have caused considerable concern since they could easily be interpreted as indications of lower standards in high schools. Harnischfeger and Wiley (1975) have subjected the evidence pertaining to nine testing pro-grammes, some of them nation-wide, to a critical review. They point out that achievement test scores in the United States increased steadily until the mid-1960s. After that many test scores—but not all of them—tended to decline. The drop has been particularly dramatic in the early 1970s and in the higher grades. It is most pronounced in verbal tests.

The Scholastic Aptitude Test shows a decline in both its verbal and mathematical scores over the past decade. The drop in verbal score is particularly marked among females. The National Assessment of Educational Progress represents an attempt to measure student competence over four-year cycles in ten subject areas among 9-, 13-, and 17-year-olds. Data are available from two occasions for science, reading, and writing mechanics. Science shows a consistent decline on all three age levels. Reading scores from two occasions are available for 17-year-olds only and show an increase over a three-year period. The outcomes in writing mechanics present a less con-sistent picture with decline at the 13- and 17-year levels and increase at the 9-year level.

Attempts to identify the factors which can account for the observed changes are beset with the difficulties indicated earlier. Since the school as the source of causes for the decline is in the focus of interest, the main problem is to try to 'partition the child's world into in- and out-of-school conditions'. The most obvious assumption from which attempts to disentangle the conditions must start is that 'out-of-school agents such as the family, television, peer groups, etc. have some effects on what pupils know and can do'. (p. 7)

School factors which deserve a close investigation as possible causes of decline are composition of enrolment, school and classroom organization, quantity of schooling, curriculum, student motivation, and characteristics of teaching staff. Certain changes in the composition of enrolment have occurred. The retention rate has increased. But neither of these two factors seems to have had any significant influence on changes in student competence. In summing up the analyses of the possible factors on the school arena, it is concluded that the 'strongest explanatory power seems to come from curricular changes'. (p. 107) There has been a considerable enrolment drop in the U.S. high school in courses in english and mathematics. Futhermore, the course enrolment decline is paralleled by a drop in mean scores. Factors such as increased retention rate and absence rate might have had some influence. The search for factors in the larger societal context is even more problematic than the one for conditions in the school arena. One could speculate about the effect of television viewing. Ninety-six per cent of homes in the United States now have television sets, and the average viewing time is close to the time students are exposed to a teacher in the classroom. Harnischfeger and Wiley hypothesize that television viewing might have different effects on children at different age levels. The verbal stimulation exerted by television plus the launching of pre-school programmes might explain why scores at the lower grades have tended to increase. Among older children, where a marked decline has occurred, television might have a contrary effect by keeping them from important educational activities, such as reading. The hypothesis is supported by evidence from the I E A survey where television viewing among 14-year-olds tends to be negatively correlated with achievements in key subject areas (see, e.g., Thorndike, 1973).

CONCLUSIONS

We are still groping in our attempts to find out about the long-term trend with regard to cognitive competence achieved by students at various grade levels. One could even question the meaningfulness of comparisons of over-time 'standards', which are products of learning conditions operating in different types of schools with different objectives and/or emphases and under sometimes radically changed societal conditions.

Representative evidence on *intellectual ability* as assessed by so-called I Q tests consistently points to a rising secular trend in Europe and the United States. In operational terms: mean scores on widely used intelligence tests have tended to increase over the fifty years that large-scale surveys have been conducted. The explanation for the increase, which invalidates the dooms-day predictions by some psychologists some decades ago, is as complicated as the entire nature–nurture problem. There are identifiable factors within the pattern of improved social condi-tions and living standards, such as nutrition and child care, the establishment of pre-schools and child-care centres, etc. Further-more, the amount of verbal stimulation provided by the mass media and—not least—by the improved formal education of parents has contributed to an enrichment which affects the performance on conventional intelligence tests.

Evidence pertaining to changes in *achievement* scores is limited almost entirely to the United States, since nation-wide achieve-ment test programmes have been rather exceptional in Europe. Harnischfeger and Wiley (1975) sum up the United States evidence as follows:

Beyond doubt, beyond differences among assessment instruments, alterations in tests, or in pupil composition, achievement test scores have been declining for about a decade in all grades from five up-wards. Score declines are more pronounced in higher grades and in recent years. They are more severe for tests probing verbal than mathematics achievements. These are the facts and they describe a National phenomenon. (pp. 115–6)

Do we need to worry about reports on declining achievement? The answer to this somewhat rhetorical question depends on two circumstances. In the first place, if the changes which, after all, are minor ones, are fluctuations depending upon temporary circumstances, such as shifts in emphasis on curricular objec-tives, there is no reason for serious concern. Secondly, the degree of concern naturally reflects the value orientation of the person involved in assessing what the schools are accomplishing.

Those who emphasize traditional objectives, plead for academic rigour, and call for 'back to the basics' of course find more reason to worry than those who conceive the educative role of the school in broader terms than that of inculcating certain academic fundamentals.

There is a cost–benefit problem here which is often overlooked. The operating costs in real terms have been rising considerably since the early 1960s. The overwhelming part of these is staff costs. The problem of whether the standards are declining or not could be secondary to the problem of utilizing staff resources for *central educative functions*. The accountability problem is not in the first place whether society gets students with formal and marketable competence worth the money it has spent on the schools, but whether the money has been spent in such a way as to promote the attainment of central educative objectives, *including* the cognitive competence instilled in the students.

7

Bureaucratization and Within-System Conflicts

CHARACTERISTICS OF BUREAUCRACY

BUREAUCRACY in the Weberian sense is an organization characterized by rationality, legality, and distribution of authority through hierarchical lines. In an analysis of bureaucracy Carl Friedrich (1963) distinguishes six elements, of which the first three apply to the relations between the members of the organization and the last three have to do with rules defining their individual behaviours.

A bureaucracy is characterized by:

(1) centralization of supervision and control,
(2) differentiation of functions,
(3) specified qualifications for office (both entry and career),
(4) objectivity (expert decisions),
(5) administrative routines, and
(6) discretion.

The 'bureaucratic problem' came to the forefront of public debate and began to be studied by social scientists after the Second World War, when both the military and civilian administrative machinery had been through a period of rapid growth and in some cases had multiplied over a few years.

A survey conducted in order to map out how people perceived bureaucracy showed that their collective experiences clustered around nine ideas (Watson, 1945). Bureaucracy was conceived as characterized by:

(1) a complicated set-up with much specialization and division of responsibility;
(2) rapid and inflexible rules with a narrow margin of adjustment to specific cases;

(3) slow operations with long delays and buck passing;
(4) duplication of efforts, waste of resources, conflict of directives;
(5) empire building of officials, efforts to magnify the authority of officials;
(6) concentration of power in the hands of a few;
(7) conflicts with democratic rights;
(8) political favouritism; and
(9) blundering and stupidity of officials.

These perceptions arise out of the frustration that the general public often experiences in its dealings with various bodies in the administrative machinery.

In the Watson study people were interviewed about what in the educational bureaucracy they found particularly burdensome. The complaints had the following components: (1) traditionalism, (2) complicated division of responsibility, (3) consequent delays in getting things done, (4) departmental empire building, (5) concentration of power at the top with helplessness at the bottom, and (6) political pull.

THREE MODELS OF EDUCATION AS AN ORGANIZATION

An incisive analysis of the educational system from the point of organizational sociology has been conducted by Michael Pusey (1976) in his book *Dynamics of Bureaucracy: A Case Analysis in Education*.

The starting point for his inquiry was the observation that bureaucratic organizations, not least the ones in education, easily become self-rigidifying, resistant to change, and thus tend to counteract their own purposes. The problem was encountered when Pusey was conducting a review of the policy and operations of the Tasmanian Department of Education in Australia. The review focused on secondary education that was thought to be lagging behind and out of phase with the surrounding society. But the main emphasis of the analysis was on the relationships between the various parts of the system: the school and its principal, the superintendent, and the State Department of Education.

The analysis considered the relationship between the operations (the work) and the type of organization. This was important since this interdependence was strongly influenced by models that the school bureaucracy tends to emulate, such as the military or the industrial one. To what extent are models of administration which emerged in military and other public agencies or industrial enterprises applicable in the educational system? Is education 'governable' in the conventional sense? Pusey separates three main aspects of an organization: its formal structure; the technology employed to achieve its aims; and its informal, social structure, the way it socializes the individuals within it. Depending upon the emphasis one can distinguish between three models of organization:

(1) the *bureaucratic* model in the Weberian sense,
(2) the *technical* model, and
(3) the *human relations* model.

Central to the bureaucratic model is the rational–legal authority and its distribution down hierarchical lines from the top to the bottom. Transactions are supposed to be performed in an impersonal, formalistic, and 'objective' way. Individuals in the organization act 'according to the book'. Members of the organization easily develop a propensity for ritualism. Particular cases or 'irritational' deviations from the behaviours foreseen in the book are abhorred. The system is built on assumptions of the *one* 'best way' of dealing with problems. A significant margin of uncertainty is supposed not to exist.

The technical model is built on the (in itself doubtful) assumption of clear distinctions between means and ends. Once the aims of the organization have been clearly specified and operationalized, the technologist steps in and points out the best method of dealing with the problem. For instance, once the goals of a certain subject area have been specified they can be translated into goal behaviours and learning processes by means of which the goals can be reached. This is the philosophy behind educational technology. The differentiation between values and facts is of course the core problem. Educational technology is built on the assumption that it is possible to operationalize perfectly the goals. This could perhaps be done in industrial training but not very successfully in education with its complex and diversified set of goals, which are immersed in subjective elements that can hardly be operationalized. Because the goals are 'inherently diffuse' a rational and operational breakdown of goals is not feasible. Such attempts exclude indeterminate and 'irrational' human factors.

Both the bureaucratic and the technical models are built on the assumption that one can 'from above' establish a rational and formal order which is followed by rational human beings. But teaching is essentially *not* a mechanical or industrial activity. It is an activity at the core of which is a personal relationship between a teacher and a student. Therefore teaching is beset with a wide margin of indeterminacy. The success of teaching depends decisively not upon the extent to which the teacher follows rules and methodological gimmicks but on his perceptiveness, intuition, and understanding; that is, on the non-formal elements that enter decisively into the teaching situation.

Thus, the potentially stressful situation between the administrator on the one side, who wants to programme what is happening in the school in a determinate and rational way, and the teacher and the students on the other side, is easily understood. The personalities of the actors in the organization constitute a margin of indeterminacy.

The human relations model recognizes the personal and social needs of the actors in the organization. The central feature is the interaction between personalities. Face-to-face communication is important. Primary needs, such as security and self-esteem, have to be satisfied. 'Effective work in indeterminate and complex professional and managerial situations requires a high emotional investment.' (p. 27)

The three features vary depending on the kind of organization under consideration. They are in tension with each other and there is no best way of organization. The degree to which the psycho-social dimension comes into the picture depends upon the degree of specificity and/or diffuseness of the tasks. The tension between the formal structure and the individual becomes more acute in organizations where values, attitudes, and emotions are vested in the tasks performed. The school is a typical organization where this is the case.

HOW BUREAUCRACY DEVELOPS IN EDUCATION

Bureaucracy defined as institutionalized rationality, uniformity of procedure, and hierarchically distributed power, has emerged concomitantly with mass education. Single schools have been merged into regional and state systems of education. The increase in size of both the individual schools and the system at all levels has called for increased co-ordination. The broadening of objectives, and the powerful role of the educational system in a meritocratic society as distributor of social status and selector for attractive positions, work in the same direction, that is to say, increase the influence of the administrative machinery.

In his analysis of educational change in the state of Massachusetts by the mid-nineteenth century Katz (1968) concludes that development in a bureaucratic direction was inevitable. The task of the school was to inculcate the basic social values of an industrial society and to serve its purposes. The main instrument for achieving this goal was the establishment of a bureaucracy.

According to a later study by Katz (1971) bureaucratization in the big cities, at least in the United States, occurred during the third quarter of the nineteenth century. He identifies three indicators of such a development, namely age-grading, introduction of a superintendent, and centralization of the school board. These changes created an increased complexity which called for co-ordination, direction, and guidance, which in their turn called for more professional supervision and specialization. Provision of professional or administrative services had to occur from central agencies through a hierarchical structure.

At the same time the process of bureaucratization offered advantages to the teachers in their quest for increased professionalism. Career lines were opened up in the administrative hierarchy. Formal rules of hiring were a protection against political discretion. The setting up of clear-cut regulations of entry into the profession and of promotion provided a certain security. The net result of bureaucratization was a more acquiescent, rule-abiding behaviour.

It is easy to conceive the development in the direction of increased bureaucratization as 'inevitable': 'Given a complex, technological society and a complex and massive social task like universal schooling, there is no other way of proceeding.' (Katz, 1971, p. XXII) But Katz maintains that industrialization *per se* does not make bureaucratization inevitable—it is inevitable only when men confront certain problems with particular values and priorities. In his view the combination of industrialization with the values of a capitalist society makes bureaucracy inevitable.

However, a comparison of school systems in socialist and capitalist or mixed-economy countries in Europe does not offer evidence that supports this view. Judging from criticisms aired in educational journals in Eastern European countries the usual drawbacks of bureaucracy do not seem to have been overcome there. As has been emphasized earlier, the system of mass production, which is at the core of industrialization, calls for regularity, standardization, and uniformity as well as the hierarchy or chain of direction and command; all of which are basic elements of the bureaucratic system.

I have elsewhere referred to this as the dilemma between meritocracy and participatory democracy:

We have on the one hand the trend toward cognitive competence becoming the 'power basis', and on the other the quest for greater equality in life chances, coping power and participation. We have on the one hand the classical liberal conception of equality which entails a belief in careers being open to talent on the basis of fair competition, and on the other the radical democratic conception according to which the distribution of abilities is an arbitrary outcome of the 'natural lottery'. We have on the one hand the strongly felt need to improve educational opportunities for those who have until now been underprivileged, and on the other the immediate demands for highly trained technological and managerial manpower. We have on the one hand a strong popular demand for an 'open door' policy in higher education, and on the other hand an often dominant element of competitiveness. We have on the one hand the 'corrective' type of egalitarianism, according to which society should confine itself to correcting for certain differences in starting chances . . .; on the other there is the 'redemptive' egalitarianism which emphasizes equality of results and is ready to distribute opportunities in a compensatory way. Evidently, the resolution of this dilemma is a matter of value priorities. The goal of economic growth is inextricably linked to the creation of competencies conducive to meritocracy. The goal of redemptive equality can be achieved only by playing down rewards, status and authority connected with superior competence. (Husén, 1974b, p. 143)

This passage should be qualified by referring to what was

suggested above. Education as a system is less prone to bureaucracy than is industry. At the core of the educational process is the interaction between a student and a teacher, which occurs with a wide margin of indeterminism, emotional involvement, and irrationality. The educational process is allergic to too much regularity, uniformity, and formality. There is no 'right way' of educating a child but many different ways which can lead to the same goal. The industrial process is by nature regular, uniform, and proceeds along prescribed tracks. Thus by its very nature the industrial process is more conducive to meritocracy and concomitantly to bureaucracy than the educational process as such.

CONSEQUENCES OF BUREAUCRACY FOR
TEACHERS AND STUDENTS

An elaborate and rigidified school bureaucracy is bound to create frustrations among the parties concerned: parents, students, and teachers. In big city school systems with a minimum of face-to-face contacts between policy-makers at the top and parents, teachers, and students at the bottom, hostility easily arises between the lay people, parents and board members, and professionals, as well as between teachers and administrators at various levels in the hierarchy.

In the mid-1950s we conducted a study of discipline in the schools of the city of Stockholm (L. Husén *et al.*, 1959) and among other things canvassed the teachers' views on school and administration. It turned out that the higher the position in the hierarchy of the administrative agency and/or official, the more frustrations and alienation were experienced in dealings with them. The school principal was accepted with certain reservations, but the attitude was more hostile towards the City Board of Education and still worse when it came to the National Board and finally to the Ministry of Education.

Resistance to reforms is a characteristic of the bureaucratic system. Reforms provide a margin of innovation but they also, particularly when initiated from above, imply a margin of insecurity. In an interesting study of teachers' attitudes towards and knowledge about the comprehensive school reform, Marklund (1961) demonstrated that the more the status of the teacher would be adversely affected by the reform, the more negative his attitude to the reform and the less he knew about it.

Another characteristic of bureaucracy is excessive uniformity and intolerance towards deviations. This is expressed in steps taken in order to enforce school attendance or the unwillingness to allow local and/or individual initiatives.

Pusey has conducted an illuminating analysis of the consequences of overemphasis on the bureaucratic dimension of an organization. In observing the actual operations in one of the state school systems in Australia he was struck by the incongruence between stated public policy and what actually happened at the school and/or classroom level. Stated goals and actual operations were very often in contradiction with each other. Similar observations have been made in studies of the administration of health care in Sweden. Stated policy of decentralization and widening of 'grassroot' initiative comes out, when implemented, as increased central control and rigidity of regulations.

Four major pervasive issues in bureaucratized educational systems can be identified:

(1) Adherence to formal rules that the actors—students, teachers, and school administrators—do not want, or dare, to abandon;

(2) Increased social distance between the strata in the system and a lack of sense of community;

(3) Relationships among strata are expressed more in terms of authority than in terms of achieving common tasks;

(4) The system is motivated more by extrinsic rewards, such as marks and salary cheques, than by intrinsic rewards, such as the joy of work or knowledge for its own sake.

The internal dynamics of the educational organization can be explained by the tensions among the three dimensions referred to earlier: the bureaucratic, the technological, and the psycho-social. This theoretical framework is useful for explaining why the stated policies so easily get thwarted.

The quest for independence easily makes adolescents perceive the status of the teacher as threatening. The threat is magnified by the authority given to the teacher. He is entitled to evaluate student performance and serve as a kind of gate-keeper to high status positions. In order to protect themselves against teacher power students tend to play the 'withdrawal game'. This game has two characteristics: (1) establishing a social distance between themselves and the teacher, and (2) falling back on formalism and rules. The withdrawal syndrome is an attempt to make oneself faceless. This reduces the margin of uncertainty but has the unintended consequence of making the system even more bureaucratic. The price paid is a loss of any genuine sense of involvement. One works only or mainly for extrinsic rewards.

The principal easily becomes a prisoner of the bureaucratic dimension, and the teacher a victim of the withdrawal game. The principal is forced to elaborate the rules and the teachers to apply them to students, a course that multiplies the disciplinary problems.

'SOLUTIONS' TO OVERBUREAUCRATIZATION

Educational policy today is faced with fundamental problems of modern society: urbanization, problems of anonymity and alienation, accelerated social change, demands of modern technology, the breaking-up of old patterns, the pressures of a consumer economy, and the effects of mass media on communication.

The obvious and immediate panacea to the problems and frustrations indicated above that even central bureaucrats fall back on is 'decentralization'. The local schools are, for instance, given greater formal discretionary power over their expenditures. But this easily leads to a new set of regulations and more administrative machinery in order to control resource utilization.

Broader solutions have to be found. Renewal is a *social* process that cannot be brought about by structural changes only. The psycho-social components have to be considered. 'Modern education and its administration can no longer be viably conceived as a mechanical activity; therefore effective change (or genuine renewal) cannot be achieved by directive or command or by efforts on the part of experts to prestructure, standardize and regulate the course of innovation.' (Pusey, 1976, p. 123)

The designer–planner's attempts to regulate the course of innovation tend to come into conflict with the partly undetermined foundations of the educational enterprise and to inhibit the exercise of professional choice.

Withdrawal or defence reactions lead, as pointed out, to more emphasis on formal authority on the part of teachers *vis-à-vis* students and administrators *vis-à-vis* teachers. When students and teachers are in a state of insecurity they easily fall back on formality as a means of protecting themselves. Thus, a vicious circle is established. The exercise of formal authority tends to harden the pattern of bureaucratic formality which further reduces the margin of initiative and of professional discretion at the classroom level, and so on. In other words, the usual panacea to problems, which are inherently bureaucratic, is to institute policies that imply more bureaucracy, such as regulations about provision of new funds and employing more staff which has then to be accommodated in the hierarchy. Bureaucracy breeds bureaucracy.

In discussing how the vicious circle could be broken it is necessary to remember that the educational process is basically an *interaction* between teachers and students, both individually and in groups, in a social context characterized by indeterminacy and thus by a need for flexibility and discretion. In some sense education is in principle 'ungovernable'. But in order to balance the bureaucratic and the psycho-social dimension of the organization the individual school has to be a supportive community which can meet the social needs of its participants. The key problem then is to make the local school into a community with wider margins for group and individual decisions and for better communication between students, teachers, principals, and parents. In sum: better conditions for interaction between the actors have to be established.

I shall later discuss in more detail what can be done to 'de-institutionalize' the school. Suffice it to point out here that smaller school units, particularly at the secondary level, are required in order to establish a spirit of community and identification. Increased participation in planning the curriculum and actual organization of the instruction at the school and classroom levels are other prerequisites. Grassroot initiatives

and innovations can be encouraged by making discretionary
funds available with a minimum of strings attached. More
discretion in recruiting staff could be left to the individual school
or school district. Less differentiation of functions will make it
possible to increase the contacts between a particular teacher
and a particular group of students.

TENS ON BETWEEN GOALS OF EQUALITY AND STATUS-DISTRIBUTIVE FUNCTIONS OF THE SCHOOL

The official policy guiding educational reforms in many countries in recent decades has been a reflection of the liberal
philosophy of an open society with equality of opportunity and
self-realization. The implementation of such a policy has been
hindered by bureaucratic constraints. Teichler (1976) has taken
Japan as an illustrative example of the tension between, on the
one hand, liberalizing and humanizing tendencies which evolve
when opportunities for furthergoing education are opened up
and, on the other hand, the selective, status-preparing functions
of the system in an industrial society. One might also view these
tensions as a conflict between the quest for self-realization and
the demands of the employment system.

The function of the school as a distributor of social positions
and roles entails two main components, namely to (1) instil a
certain level of competency appropriate for the working life,
and (2) distribute social status. When opportunities are broadened, there is a tendency to require more formal education
which then is regarded as something worthwhile in itself. The
status-distributive function is evident in a meritocratic framework of education wherein everybody, through the removal of
formal or economic barriers, is free to compete and prove himself. The broadening of opportunities, moreover, will contribute
to increasing democracy by providing the insights and the common frame of reference which are conducive to participatory
democracy.

The notion of a 'fundamental harmony' between individual
aspirations and social requirements (including the demands of
the employment system) has proven false. It was based upon
the questionable notion of a pre-established harmony between
individual aspirations and the structure of the employment

system. By diagnosing correctly everybody's interests and abilities it would be possible to arrange for everybody to get the position and status that suited his assets.

But, instead of allowing the individual more scope to develop his own abilities and bents, the increase in enrolment at advanced stages and the levelling-out of differences in amount of formal education have led to an inflation of educational requirements on the part of the employment system. At the same time the status differences both in working life and in society at large lead to two consequences that Teichler illustrates with the Japanese example:

(*a*) The role of the educational system as a selector becomes increasingly intense: there is a recurrent, reinforced tendency on the part of the employment system to look at the school as a selector and a distributor of status.

(*b*) The curricular content becomes increasingly irrelevant and the teaching increasingly ritualistic.

Further, tensions have become apparent over the last few years in Europe, for instance in the Federal Republic of Germany and Sweden:

(1) Doubts have been expressed about the need for highly qualified manpower to the extent that was anticipated at the beginning of the 1960s. This has generated resistance toward further expansion of the educational system.

(2) The status expectations of the students can hardly be harmonized with the existing social status structure, since more education leads to more criticism of the existing social order and the hierarchical structure of working life.

(3) Scepticism is voiced about compensatory education, the effect of integrated schooling, and the removal of selection and admissions barriers.

(4) The legal and administrative machinery set up for selection has increasingly become the focus of controversy; as, e.g., the *numerus clausus* debate in Germany (on limited admission to university programmes) or the 'total dimensioning' of enrolment in higher education proposed in Sweden.

The report by the U68 Commission in Sweden (S O U, 1973) illustrates the tendencies indicated here. Quite obviously, the administrative machinery and not the content of higher education was in the foreground of the Commission's deliberations.

Admittedly, the needs of working life were strongly emphasized and the reform was launched as a 'working-life oriented' one, with representatives of the labour market organizations on the regional boards and the curriculum committees of the universities. But the idea of advanced education for self-fulfilment and self-realization was beyond the Commission's horizon. This accounts for the strong resistance to the recommendations among both university teachers and students, particularly the latter.

A consequence of increased competition on the basis of the amount of formal education as described by Thurow (1972) is that the content of education increasingly becomes less important, whereas the formal requirements are continuously brought into focus. The substantive content of 'qualifications' for a particular occupation becomes less and less important. Educational and vocational motives are yielding to status-motives. When a society is on the verge of mass higher education, the status-distributive function of the system comes into the foreground, whereas the task of imparting specific skills becomes of less importance.

Teichler's central thesis is that the tendency up to the stage of mass higher education towards a closer connection between education and occupation in both status-distributive and content-qualification respects has come to an end. We are now facing a 'reversal of tendency' which not only leads to a gradual dissolution of this connection but also to an increased demand on the educational system, in spite of the substantial levelling-out of formal education, to prepare the students for social inequality. The frictions which emerge in connection with fitting education to working life as well as within the educational system when it comes to assigning ranks (marking) thus become a central problem for educational policy. The selection problem becomes the paramount problem in societies with mass education at advanced (upper secondary and university) levels.

The competition mechanisms work something like this. More students, of different categories, gain access to advanced education. At the same time status differences in society prevail and success in school still depends to a large extent on social background. This looms large in an educational system which is increasingly perceived as, and which is in the process of becoming more and more, an institution for social selection. Eventually, the 'selection pressure' becomes dominant and the content of education is pushed to the background.

Japan offers an illustration of the new scholasticism and of the role played by formal education in individual socio-economic careers. Success in education determines later life chances. Therefore, young people do all that they can in order to succeed and compete in the educational arena. In recruiting entrants to an occupation scholastic success is the most important criterion. The ranking of entrants applies both to the public and private sector. Because of life-long employment and promotion according to seniority the initial differences are preserved. The decisive period of three years covers transition to senior secondary school and transition to university which are characterized by an institutional hierarchy of prestige.

CONTRADICTIONS BETWEEN GOAL RHETORIC AND ADMINISTRATIVE REGULATIONS

Contradictory demands on the school give rise to conflicts and frustrations. The gap between goal rhetoric, what the school is supposed to achieve, and the resources and conditions conducive of attaining these goals has tended to widen. There is in the achievement-oriented society an inherent conflict between the humanistic ideal of self-realization with child-centred instruction and the hierarchically structured administrative machinery. The conflict between the goal system and the system of regulations is fundamental. The reason is that the goal system is horizontally structured—it implies work *with* those concerned in the system, whereas the regulation system is vertically structured—it 'talks down' *to* the representatives of the system.

The explicit aim of the goal system is individual self-realization. The rule system, however, aims at producing competent citizens for the various slots in the labour market. On the one hand the school is expected to implement goals of a democratic and anti-authoritarian character; on the other hand it is, like private and public business, part of a huge bureaucracy, which is governed from the top down.

The conflict between the two systems has serious consequences for methods of instruction, evaluation of student progress, and the way the teacher and student roles are played. The curriculum gives large margins of freedom to the teacher, but centrally approved textbooks and other teaching material decisively influence the actual teaching. Local schools and individual teachers have, according to the rhetoric, full freedom, but in reality the rules bind the teacher by means of centrally prepared teaching material, examinations, and tests.

Co-operation amongst teachers, for instance team teaching, amongst students in group work, and between teachers and students, is hampered by regulations which have been agreed on by the central officials of the teacher associations and government agencies. Co-operation must be based on partners of equal footing, but the entire system is embedded in a hierarchical structure with a climate of competition.

8

Secondary Education and 'Preparation for Life'

THE CHANGING ROLE OF THE TEENAGER

THE social role of the teenager in highly industrialized societies has over a few decades undergone a profound alteration. The most striking change is that the great majority of the teenagers today are found in the schools and not at the work places. In Europe before 1950 only a small social and intellectual élite of less than twenty per cent of the teenage cohort proceeded in full-time schooling beyond completion of mandatory schooling at 13 or 14. Until not very long ago the school essentially fulfilled two major functions, both auxiliary and supplementary to the family, where the major educational functions took place. (1) The élite, many of them destined for the professions, early entered separate schools (grammar school, *gymnasium*, *lycée*) in order to obtain the proper grounding for further education preparatory to high-status occupations. (2) The great majority, according to legislation on compulsory elementary education, entered schools where they were taught the three Rs and sometimes also the Scriptures. These two school systems fitted an ascriptive society where education and social background were almost perfectly correlated.

The 1940s saw a breakthrough in the notion of equal opportunity. According to this doctrine educational status and subsequent social status were to be achieved rather than ascribed; that is, were to reflect 'genuine' aptitude. This was in essence the philosophy of *freie Bahn den Tüchtigen*. Universal secondary education was already being provided in the economically more developed parts of the United States in the 1920s and 1930s. It began to be introduced in the more affluent and/or industrialized

European countries after the war. The Education Act in England in 1944, the French decree of 1959, the Swedish acts on comprehensive education in 1950 and 1962 are cases in point. Statistics show in detail how the 'enrolment explosion' hit one stage of the educational system after the other (OECD, 1971a and UNESCO, 1974). The exponential increase first occurred at the lower secondary level, then, with a time lag of a few years, at the upper secondary level, and, with a further lag, finally reached the university level. The inflow of students broke all forecasts, which then notoriously tended to be on the conservative side. Partly because of legislation raising the mandatory school leaving age and partly because of the increased number of young people who proceed to upper secondary school, some European countries are now rapidly approaching the point where the great majority of young people in the age range 15 to 20 (as is already the case in the United States) are found in school.

When in 1928 I completed the six-year elementary school, which then represented the entire mandatory school attendance, the great majority—in fact almost 90 per cent—of the 13-year-olds in Sweden left school in order to join the ranks of the adult world. Only one out of ten went to junior secondary school. When I entered upper secondary school, I represented one out of twenty in the age group. Only one out of fifty entered university after matriculation examination. Today, when the mandatory school leaving age is 16, there is provision in the upper secondary school for some 90 per cent of the 16–17-year-olds. One out of four enter institutions of higher education.

Concomitantly with the expanded enrolment the school as an institution has been assigned functions which previously were discharged by the home and/or the work place. Instead of entering the adult world to learn adult roles, the teenagers find themselves in institutions where they have limited contact with adult society. We are witnessing a large-scale age segregation.

It is striking to note that together with the increased number of years of formal schooling goes a tendency to shelter the students from adult responsibilities and to create conditions supportive of enlarged student roles. Young people are cut off from productive work under what have been referred to as prison-like constraints. The schools have become bigger, and the typical teenager in Europe today is 'processed' in a school plant that typically accommodates about one thousand of his peers. The expansion of the organization means less personal contact and more bureaucratic formality. The school-day is chopped up into uniform periods and breaks according to the clock. What goes on in the classroom is prepared in detail. The methods of instruction are dominated by the classical 'frontal instruction' that assumes passive absorption on the part of the student. He is more or less systematically shielded from responsibility, and he often learns only too perfectly to become irresponsible. Some twenty years ago I coined the phrase 'functional participation' to indicate work practices conducive to the development of student responsibility and social maturity. In a report submitted on a study of school discipline it was pointed out that we cannot expect young people who leave school to be capable of more responsibility than the school has allowed them to acquire (**L. Husén,** 1959)

SOCIAL CHANGES CONDUCIVE TO YOUTH PROBLEMS

What social changes have been conducive to the problems of youth? An important issue is, as pointed out above, the segregation of youth from other age groups and, hence, from the wider society. Largely because of extended schooling young people have become increasingly separated from adults. There is less contact than before between the growing generation and their elders in the family. Even within the various age categories there is increased separation with less contact among children belonging to different age groups, even within the same family. The way school is organized in stages and grades establishes barriers between youngsters at various age levels.

Segregation means setting up barriers between generations and/or between main societal domains, such as between education and working life. Young people are more or less banned from access to certain responsible work tasks. But in other respects a wider range of options has been opened up. In leisure-time activities and in terms of consumption patterns young people now have more options than in earlier days.

Another aspect is that young people grow up in a society where they meet adults in segmented contexts and in specialized roles, for example, at pre-school age in day-care centres. Instead of being in continuous contact with one adult or a group of adults they only have opportunities for intermittent, instant contacts. Such experiences become further reinforced as they move through the school, when they are taught the various subjects by specialized teachers and are being treated by specialists in medical care, social work, and the like. For young people this pattern of fragmented contacts is detrimental to the development of stable emotional relationships with adults, including their parents.

A third major issue relates to the widened role and scope of formal schooling. The common school was originally established to transmit certain skills and knowledge. In our present society the school is, as the Panel on Youth puts it, 'inherently ill-suited' to fulfil other functions in preparing for adult life yet is expected to do so. 'Schools are apart from society while the non-academic portions of becoming adult, such as gaining the capacity to take responsibility and authority, learning to care for others who are dependent, acquiring the ability to take decisive action, learning how to work, achieving a sense of self-respect, are directly part of society.' (Coleman *et al.*, 1974, p. 142) The essential drawback of the contemporary school, when it comes to socializing young people into adult responsibilities, is that it makes the student altogether a dependant.

OVERARCHING PROBLEMS IN TRANSITION FROM YOUTH TO ADULTHOOD

Young people are today caught in a squeeze between many conflicting forces. They mature biologically one to two years earlier than did their counterparts some fifty years ago but they stay longer in school and assume important adult responsibilities much later. There is also a lack of consistency in how young people are treated: in some countries at the age of 18 they have the right to vote but not the right to participate in decision-making in their educational institutions. They want to establish adult identity as holders of occupations but are not wanted at the work places. They do not want to stay on in a school with all the pressures for achievement and irrelevance of curriculum, but are fully aware that the number of educational credentials they can amass determines their subsequent careers. The greater the number of students who pursue studies in order to achieve higher qualifications, the stronger the tendency to enhance entrance requirements to many occupations. A recent Australian report (Wright and Headlam, 1976) about the educationally disadvantaged talks about the 'malaise within the education processes themselves' and the sacrifice of genuine educational values that occurs under such conditions.

What ways out of the squeeze could be considered? Analysts agree that the drawbacks of postponed adulthood in terms of taking responsibilities and duties and assuming independence must in one way or another be alleviated. But most of the time increased participation and assumption of democratic responsibilities have been contemplated only for the schools which thereby become a kind of social sanctuary. As has been pointed out above, admission into the world of adult pursuits has been barred because young people are not accepted as fully-fledged workers in a society with a highly rationalized and profit-oriented labour market. The first to leave school are those who come from less school-conscious homes. This further increases inequalities in life chances among social strata.

FAILURE OF SECONDARY SCHOOL TO PREPARE FOR ADULT RESPONSIBILITIES

Formal schooling today covers a longer period in a person's life and has taken over socializing functions which previously were handled in adult settings, such as at the work place. But the school with its present institutional structure and resources has not been able with prospects of success to shoulder the new responsibilities. Hence the 'crisis', particularly in secondary schools which are on a collision course with society. We must take new bearings in order to make the appropriate course corrections to avoid the collision.

The criticism of the school as a socializing agent by all who have looked thoroughly into the matter has been extremely harsh. Silberman (1970) finds that secondary schools tend to transmit values of 'docility, pacifity, conformity, and lack of trust'. (p. 159) The Kettering Commission (Brown *et al.*, 1973) on the reform of secondary education finds education 'warped by the tension between a rapidly changing society and a slowly changing school'. (p. 3) The Panel on Youth (Coleman *et al.*, 1974) talks about 'alienation from the rest of the society and lack of motivation to enter adult life'. (p. 3) The U.S. Office of Education (USOE) panel points out that in spite of young people maturing physically two years earlier than a couple of generations ago, they are kept in a prolonged dependency in school. 'As a result, we have succeeded in producing a youth society housed in overburdened institutions excessively isolated from the reality of the community and the adult world.' The USOE panel uses a striking metaphor in saying that 'we have used our schools, inadvertently, as the social "aging vats" that have isolated adolescents and delayed their learning adult roles, work habits, and skills' (Martin *et al.*, 1974, p. 10).

The problems indicated above began to be investigated some twenty years ago. Pioneering studies of the 'adolescent society' were conducted by James Coleman (1961), who set out to study the 'value climate' in secondary schools and to assess the relative influence of the home, the school, and the peer group on that climate. Coleman came to the conclusion that teenagers were segregated from the rest of the society for reasons indicated above. He further found that the peer group was competing with parents in exercising a socializing influence and that the school (represented by the teachers) was at a disadvantage in that respect. The 'generation gap' in value orientation implied in such findings has, as we shall see, been challenged.

In the early 1970s Coleman chaired a Panel on Youth (Coleman *et al.*, 1974). The panelists were drawn from a wide range of disciplines, such as history, psychology, sociology, and anthropology. The mandate was simply to explore what kind of learning environments in present-day society could best facilitate the transmission to maturity; that is, help them to become adults. The Report of the Panel points out that in agrarian society young people learned at home what they needed to know in order to fulfil their adult roles in working life. The school served only as a supplement. But in modern society, where young people increasingly (presently in 80–95 per cent of the cases) end up in occupations different from those of their parents, a long period of specialized preparation is necessary in order to enable them to function satisfactorily as adults. Separate institutions have to be relied on to accomplish these tasks. The task of making young people psychologically and socially mature has to a large extent been turned over to the school. Increasingly, the home tends to be closed down during the day. The Report points out:

Our basic premise is that the school system, as now constituted, offers an incomplete context for the accomplishment of many important facets of maturation. The school has been well designed to provide some kinds of training but, by virtue of that fact, is inherently ill-suited to fulfill other tasks essential to the creation of adults. (Coleman *et al.*, 1974, p. 2)

Coleman has described the problem with a catchphrase: the school is 'information-rich' but 'action-poor'. The school is a place where conceptual and verbal skills are taught but where little concrete action can take place. The realities of the outer world are dealt with by abstract verbal media. To be sure, this is the real strength of the school. Abstract concepts and verbal tools are indispensable in enabling young people to cope intellectually and technically with the surrounding world. But the weakness is the tendency to make the verbal–abstract exercise an end in itself, something that is further strengthened by the ritualism of marks and examinations. The one who successfully masters the rituals is rewarded, while the one who is able to apply what he has learnt is not. B. F. Skinner has sarcastically remarked that the American student who in impeccable French can say, 'Please pass me the salt', gets an A, whereas his French counterpart who utters the same words gets the salt!

In considering the role of the school in society today Coleman (1974) makes the following observations.

Young people are obtaining the information that constitutes their cognitive competence either from direct or from vicarious experience. In the former case they are observers, passive and/or active. In the latter case they are *told* about something they do not have an opportunity to observe directly or they can *read* about it. Schools were once, in an 'information-poor society', designed to provide some necessary vicarious experience. These conditions have in our time been radically changed by mass media and travel. Society has now in several respects become 'information-rich', in contrast to the old static rural and 'information-poor' society.

When schools were set up, they held a monopoly not only on information but also on how to select the non-experiential information that was imparted. This power to select according to certain values, usually religious ones, made it possible for the school to shape students' values effectively. Readers and *abcdaires* were also used in order to convey moral notions and religious beliefs.

The school in the Western world today is in principle committed to pluralism in terms of values, views, and sources of information. In contrast to traditional schooling, the contemporary stated objective is to make the students critical and thus enable them to arrive independently at conclusions and beliefs. This heavily reduces the school's power to select and to shape attitudes and views.

The school is promotive of individualism. There is little opportunity for collective action among students, whether called group work or not. The individualistic trend has been reinforced by the school serving as a screening device for working life. This is the main power left to the school. The growing importance of credentials and amount of formal education necessary for gaining a favourable place in the line of employment-seekers has intensified competition and increased the power of the institution whose prime role has become that of serving as a gatekeeper to the world of work and an assigner of social status.

CHALLENGED EVIDENCE ON YOUTH CULTURE

I have several times cited *Youth: Transition to Adulthood*, the report submitted by the Panel on Youth of the President's Science Advisory Committee (Coleman *et al.*, 1974). The main characteristics of the youth culture according to the Panel are:

Inward-lookingness

Young people in the highly industrialized and affluent society largely turn to one another to form a kind of self-contained youth culture. This is reflected in the tendency to be both consumers and producers of, for instance, distinctive types of music and clothing. Such a development has been furthered by prolonged formal schooling, by increasing standards of living that make young people important buyers, and by the very fact that they have until recently been numerous. Living together in communes is an illustration of the inward-lookingness and the physical attachment of young people to their own age group. Family cohesiveness has diminished, the stronger the attachment to peers has become.

Press Toward Autonomy

The Panel notes the increased deviation of youth norms from those of adults as a consequence of the fact that for some youth prestige among their peers is dependent upon direct confrontation with adults—frequently by challenging the values and conventions of adult society. Peer group cultures have been able to maintain a relatively autonomous patterning because of the diversification of the mass media which can make certain subgroups their targets.

Concern for the Underdog

Young people increasingly express their sympathies for the Third World or for ethnic minorities within their own countries. Such reactions are inspired by the feeling of being outsiders themselves.

Interest in Change

The question for radical overhaul, or even overturn, is also inspired by the feeling of being outsiders. As society has become increasingly achievement-oriented with status allocation depending on individual achievements, and with reaction against this on the part of the youth, conflict easily occurs.

The evidence presented in support of the Report of the Panel and its recommendations has been challenged in three respects. The very conceptualization of youth culture and the alienation of youth in industrialized mass-education society has been challenged by neo-Marxist scholars (see, e.g., Behn *et al.*, 1974) who maintain that the alienation and tension between the school and the adolescents are not due to lack of congruence or a disjunction between the school as an institution and the world of work. On the contrary, in a mass production and consumption society young people are simply revolting against being indoctrinated and manipulated. Furthermore, in preparing a docile work-force the school performs a sifting and sorting function which conflicts with individual aspirations for self-development and personal fulfilment.

The validity of adolescent attitudes and reactions as described by Coleman and his Panel has also been challenged. It has been maintained, for example, that the picture given in his studies of the youth culture and in the Panel report reflects the reactions and attitudes of upper or upper-middle class youngsters in the United States. Andersson (1969), who conducted a longitudinal survey of all grade 8 and grade 9 comprehensive school students in the city of Gothenburg, found that the value orientation of students toward parents, peers, and teachers in terms of preferences was almost identical with the one reported by Coleman from ten high schools in Iowa. However, the value orientation varied depending upon the domain under investigation. In some cases young people are most influenced by the values of their peers but in others by the values of their parents. There was no support for a *consistent* 'generation gap' in the sense that young people throughout tend to be oriented towards the values of their peers.

In an evaluation of several reports on youth problems conducted by the Rand Corporation (Timpane *et al.*, 1976) questions were raised as to the validity of generalizations about the 'disjunctions' and 'gaps' between the generations and to what extent there actually is such a marked segregation as depicted in the report of the Panel. Statistics about labour-force participation between 1947 and 1974 do not seem to indicate delayed entry into the important sector of the adult world that consists of work. But other evidence lends support to the Panel's contention of an increased segregation.

Even the question whether there is any 'youth problem' at all has been raised. This might seem strange considering the upheavals of the 1960s and the rise of delinquency and drug abuse. The 'trouble-oriented' approach to youth problems has been the predominant one. Adolescence has traditionally been regarded as a period of disjunctions and discontinuity in the life-cycle. Phrases such as 'generation gap' and 'storm and stress' have been used in order to catch what appear to be salient features of that period. Those who spearheaded the youth revolt, who downgraded traditional values, and who challenged authority, have been perceived as typical representatives of their generation, whereas their role has mainly been that of 'forerunners'.

Unfortunately, rather limited representative evidence is available on young people's attitudes and values as compared with those of their parents. Evidence on how values and attitudes change from one generation of young people to the next is even more scarce. To my knowledge the only source of information in the latter respect consists of the Yankelovich surveys on American youth from 1967 onwards. These and other surveys tell us that the talk about generation gaps could be rather misleading. For instance, the 'gap' between upper-middle class youngsters and their parents was at the end of the 1960s much less developed than that between them and conservative people of *all* other generations. Surveys show that the within-generation variability is much larger than that between generations. Thus social class and/or educational background are of the utmost importance in determining young people's perceptions, attitudes, and behaviours with regard, for instance, to education and work. Disenchantment with school takes on a different character among youngsters from educated homes with verbal articulation than among those from deprived homes brought up in verbal poverty. The unemployment rate among 16–18-year-olds in some countries is 3–4 times higher than among those who go to school until the age of twenty, which is bound to have repercussions on the attitudes of the two groups.

Youth can, however, be conceived as a period of *both* reproduction and transformation. Young people become socialized by their family, their school, and their peers. By and large they internalize the prevailing values of these agents. The preponderance of one of them over the others varies among generations and social strata. But socialization is not 'perfect' in the sense that the young indiscriminately accept the values of the previous generation. There is always a margin of freedom in the *selection* of values which guide the socialization process, chiefly among the more articulate young people who most frequently are found in the youth movement. They are forerunners who herald new paradigms of thought and new valuations. As can be seen from the Yankelovich (1974) surveys, the new values then spread to the larger mass of young people. For instance, in the

late 1960s the challenge to the traditional work ethic was confined almost entirely to campus youth, whereas in the early
1970s, when the work ethic became more strict on campus, it
tended to slacken among the rest of the youth generation.

CHANGING VALUES AMONG YOUTH

A change in values over the last decade has been noticeable in
the more affluent societies. Once basic material needs have
been satisfied, certain other values begin to gain in relative
importance. Somewhat schematically it can be said that
expressive values have gained in importance relative to instrumental ones. A change towards expressive values can be traced
behind the quest among articulated youth for a better quality of
life, the increased emphasis on spiritual and humanistic pursuits, and the opposition to positivism, pragmatism, and
technology.

In trying to assess the changing values of American youth
Yankelovich (1972) makes a distinction between 'forerunners'
and 'practically-minded'. According to Havighurst's (1975)
estimation, the forerunners make up some 20 per cent of the age
group 15 to 25. They are more frequently dissenting with their
parents about social and political issues, they want social
changes that would play down the consumption society, and
they emphasize artistic values and self-expression. The 'dis-
senters' and 'young radicals' in Keniston's (1971) terms constitute a sub-group of the forerunners. They are oriented
towards expressive values. They want to use their education as
an instrument of criticizing society rather than as a means of
perpetuating a growth-oriented, technological society. The
practically-oriented, on the other hand, who in Havighurst's
estimation constitute some 60 per cent of the youth of 15 to 25,
are 'the apprentices to the leaders of the technocratic,
production-oriented, instrumental society' (Havighurst and
Drever, 1975, p. 142). They endorse values of productivity,
achievement motivation, materialism, and social responsibility
(law and order). The rest consist of some 20 per cent of 'left-
outs', who are the less educated and less articulated and who
are recruits of the 'new under-class'.

We are here dealing with ideal types. A dichotomy between

'forerunners' and 'practically-minded' or between expressively-
oriented and instrumentally-oriented does not, of course, exist
in reality. But the value characteristics described tend to cluster
in the two syndromes described, which makes the distinction
between the two types heuristically useful. It helps us to understand the reactions among young people towards education, the
way their performances are evaluated, and what they expect
from their working life.

CHANGING ATTITUDES TO EDUCATION AND WORK

Since systematic, and in particular comparative, evidence
covering a long period is lacking, it is hard to judge how significant the changes are in attitudes towards education and work
that have taken place among various categories of young people.
Student activism on questions of marks, examinations, and
participation in decision-making are symptoms of such a
change. Confrontations between students and decision-making
bureaucracies are other indications. Disregarding occasional
and local eruptions, one can trace what could fittingly be called
a 'quiet revolution' inspired by values and attitudes on the basis
of which redefinitions of work, success, and quality of life have
taken place.

It should, however, again be underscored that the proponents
of what in a Yankelovich (1974) survey is referred to as 'the
New Values' are more pronounced among the better educated
and articulate youngsters. But these values are in the process of
spreading to the entire youth generation.

Some of the salient features of the changing value pattern are:

(1) The notion of a successful career as a continuous advancement and promotion in a process of selection and competition,
where the able and ambitious succeed and the others fail, are
rejected. More emphasis is placed on self-fulfilment, security,
and development of rewarding leisure-time interests. Intrinsic
satisfaction increasingly tends to be preferred to instrumental
satisfaction in both education and work. One typical objection
against relative school marks, which rank students, is that they
make students work for marks and not for the rewards ensuing
from the acquisition of true education and self-developing
competencies.

(2) Education should attempt to attain the wider range of objectives that are mentioned in the rhetoric of Education Acts, preambles to curricula, and graduation speeches. Studies are not for narrow vocational goals only, but for the development of the whole personality. The overarching purpose of education at any stage is to prepare the individual to become a creative and participating citizen. Reforms of, for instance, higher education advanced under the auspices of an enrolment explosion, limited resources, and 'management of decline', have aimed at making university programmes narrowly defined in vocational competencies. Such reforms or reform proposals in, for instance, Sweden and France, have been strongly rejected by the students who resent being 'prepared for vocational slots'. They do not resent study programmes that are linked to action—the enthusiasm which has met cross-disciplinary programmes focusing on major social problems bears witness to this. But they want a better balance to be struck between humanistic education and practical preparation. Above all: the resentment is strong against programmes which lead to specific occupational competence, because of the fear of being locked into a particular occupation with limited leeway for a career change. They want education to prepare them for a broad range of (largely unforeseen) tasks that they might encounter in a dynamic society where the individual wants to have more freedom over his career decisions.

(3) There is a growing tendency among young people, who are reacting against competition and credentialism, to conceive education as something that in the future can be 'mixed' into the career pattern in different ways. The mounting number of students who do not any longer take their entire formal education *en bloc*, but 'stop out' for a certain period before proceeding with, for instance, university studies, is an important symptom of changed attitudes. Credentialism and bureaucratization are perceived as mutually reinforcing agents which together account for the rigidities and lack of flexibility which bar educational reforms.

(4) Concomitant with the rapidly rising level of formal education among entrants to the world of work, and to a large extent an outcome of it, is a profound change occurring in the perception of what work means. We have already pointed out

the trend towards emphasis on intrinsic instead of instrumental or extrinsic satisfaction. As is shown by surveys conducted over the last decade, for instance by Yankelovich (1974), middle and upper-middle class youngsters tend increasingly to strive for intrinsic rewards, whereas the lower class and less educated favour more instrumental ones—but the gap between the two groups is narrowing, which is another indication of 'the New Values' spreading from privileged and more articulate groups to the entire youth generation.

(5) The quest for self-fulfilment and meaningfulness applies to work as well as to education. This is part of what has repeatedly been referred to as the 'revolution of rising expectations'. Young people increasingly want to hold jobs which allow them a certain margin of freedom in terms of personal initiative. They want to have more say about the working conditions and the planning of the work process. They do not accept the drudgery and boredom which their elders had to put up with.

(6) There is today a marked tendency among young people all over the industrialized world to postpone the time when they feel it appropriate to 'settle down'. One leading American vocational guidance expert, Donald Super, who has followed up youngsters from the beginning of high school through their twenties, talks about a stage of 'floundering' in the development of vocational maturity. Kerr (1977) suggests that one should distinguish between two stages of youth development: adolescence and young adulthood. The former ends at the age of 17–18, when a considerable number leave school, and the other changes, with a less distinct boundary, into adulthood about the age of 25.

(7) The division of labour has often been taken as something given, with the task of the educational system to prepare every individual for his slot in the world of work. But 'over-education' among young people in the wake of the enrolment explosion tends to affect the working life in several respects. The average and considerably raised level of general education affects the docility of workers and the acceptance of what superiors are doing and ordering. Quests for participation in decision-making about the working milieu and in production process arise (O'Toole, 1977). The hierarchical division of labour tends to

change when employees are represented on various decision-making bodies in an enterprise, such as the Board (Levin, 1977).

The rapidly increasing availability of non-mandatory further education has, as we have seen, caused rising expectations and aspirations. These include hopes about the status and the nature of jobs to which additional schooling and the ensuing credentials will entitle those who 'stick it out'.

Young people and their parents are intensely aware of the role played by the formal system of education in determining an individual's future social role and job status. Therefore, even those who hold quite negative attitudes about the content of education offered by the institutions they attend are ready to embark on long courses of study. They realize perfectly well that the amount of formal education they have covered will decide the place they will occupy both in the line of applicants for entry to the next level of schooling and finally in the line of job seekers. They are also aware of the fact that, in spite of much recent talk about 'over-education' and unemployment among university graduates, holders of basic degrees are much less likely to become unemployed than are secondary school leavers or drop-outs.

In the IEA twenty-country survey, student attitudes toward schooling as well as toward success in school were assessed (Husén *et al.*, 1973). Students from industrialized and affluent countries, such as Sweden and the Federal Republic of Germany, scored low on the Like School scale, whereas students in developing countries with miserable school facilities scored high. The most reasonable explanation—lacking further evidence—that can be advanced is that in affluent countries there are too many other agents that compete with the school, such as media, sports, and other leisure-time activities. But since the negativism tends to increase during the last few years of mandatory school attendance, another explanation is the growing awareness among young people of circumstances that frustrate their hopes and aspirations.

The other attitude measure in the IEA survey was School Motivation. The attitude scale was based on questions such as 'Do you consider it important that you perform well in school?' This score tended to increase as the students moved up through the grades, which on the surface might seem strange, since the general attitude towards schooling went down. But considering the indisputable fact that in countries with low Like-School scores the majority of students voluntarily proceed beyond the completion of mandatory schooling, the contradiction becomes more apparent than real. The importance of formal education for selection in the job market and the career prospects that go with it constitute enough extrinsic motivation to 'stick it out'.

A minority of leavers, who give up even before completing the mandatory schooling stage, often regard school attendance from 13 to 16 as equivalent to an extended gaol term. This is further evidenced in many countries by truancy statistics.

In spite of much rhetoric to the contrary, excessive credentialism seems to be still gaining ground (Teichler, 1976; Dore, 1976). The idyllic picture of young people who, after careful guidance and on the basis of realization of their 'real abilities and bents', successively approach the occupational domain and the specific job of their personal choice, contrasts with the grim reality facing many youngsters, namely that of negative choice made for them by school at an early stage of their education.

The intense, not to say aggressive, debate in recent years among young people about school marks, examinations, and *numerus clausus* reflects a revolt against credentialism among articulate (and vociferous) students. In several European countries student leaders at both secondary and tertiary levels have come out strongly against the relative marking system in which students are compared with each other on the basis of norms derived from the distribution of performances in the entire student population. In many cases the reaction has been against all kinds of individual examinations and the opponents have demanded group examinations instead. The preference for so-called criterion-referenced tests and examinations, where some kind of absolute mastery has been defined and where the ranking of students has to yield to a division into passes and failures, has to be viewed in this context.

Questions like at what stages and by means of what techniques marks should be given have in recent years become major educational issues in several countries. In Sweden, these issues largely account for the fervent participation of young people in their student associations. The National Board of Education, as well as a commission of inquiry into the matter appointed by the government, have come out in favour of marks being given at crucial points in the career of students when there is a need to assess them in terms of their performance for the next stage. These decision points are at the end of mandatory schooling and at the end of the senior secondary school. The main argument in favour of keeping a system of school marks is the need for prospective employers to assess the relative qualifications of job seekers. Marks are used in the first place to select the best qualified, when the number of applicants exceeds the number of places available in a particular course. Thus, they are used in selecting students who proceed from the comprehensive school to one of the some twenty tracks and programmes in the *gymnasium*, the upper secondary stage. Students who proceed straight from *gymnasium* to university—they still constitute a majority of entrants into institutions of higher education—are competing mainly on the basis of the marks they have managed to acquire.

No doubt the emotional fire in the debate on school marks in countries which have gone through the enrolment explosion stage is fuelled by the fact that marks are instruments of competition. What appears to be a small but strong minority of students fights against marks because changes in values over the last ten years have had repercussions on a broad range of issues in the political domain. Marks are conceived as instruments of the capitalist, free market society, where the ruling class tries to utilize the educational system for its purposes, namely, as a criterion for 'slotting' people into the employment system, without consideration of intrinsic educational values. The sorting performed by the school is seen as subservience to labour market forces. It is also pointed out that the marking and ranking of individual performances is not compatible with the values expressed in curricular rhetoric on education for co-operation and self-fulfilment.

It should, however, be kept in mind that opinion about the marking and ranking system is highly divided among students. There are indications that a majority of students would prefer marks to other types of individual assessment. The problem is that the majority tends to be more silent than the active minority. One could venture the diagnosis that the attitudes of the less vociferous majority are rather pragmatic. The reality of meritocracy is there. The school alone cannot do away with it, simply because it is not operating in a social vacuum. I have previously (Husén, 1974b) raised the question: to what extent is a meritocratic component inherently necessary in the social fabric of industrialized societies, and are the drawbacks of meritocracy a necessary price that one has to pay for keeping the machinery running and the economy growing?

EFFECTS OF CREDENTIALISM AND COMPETITION

I have pointed out that education in modern, industrialized societies is faced with what appears to be a paradox. Increased opportunity in terms of vastly increased numbers in secondary and higher education goes hand in hand with a fiercely increased competition. How can we account for this paradox? Teichler, Hartung, and Nuthmann (1976), in a study for I L O of the expansion of higher education and the need for manpower, advance the following explanation. The transformation from an élite to a mass system of education at the secondary and tertiary levels tends to put into question the legitimacy of hierarchically structured social distinctions and the reward system that goes with it. Therefore steps are taken by the ruling élite to protect these distinctions and the associated privileges. 'Over-education' is avoided by raising the entry qualifications into the world of work. In addition, there has been a call for putting on the brakes, particularly on university expansion, with reference to the manpower needs.

The 'malaise within the educational processes themselves which must be taken seriously' stems from the frustrations of the hopes and aspirations of young people. It has, for instance, been dealt with by a 'Report on Poverty, Education and Adolescents' presented to the Australian Government in 1975. The Report succinctly points out certain basic dilemmas which are shared by many highly industrialized countries. It points at the forces (indicated above) that have been creating a need for more and more formal education. The result has been a need for expanded basic schooling and higher and higher academic qualifications. At the same time there has been a trend towards higher entrance qualifications for most occupations. This has put increased pressure on young people to remain in school, irrespective of whether or not what they learn is relevant to their personal needs and development.

Depth interviews with a cross-section of 18-year-olds indicate that there is a 'serious dissonance' between what the youngsters expect to gain from their education and what they actually get. Furthermore there is a clear-cut lack of congruence between what they hope to derive and what representatives of the authorities value.

The Australian report is not the sole witness about basic dilemmas in secondary education. The report *Youth: Transition to Adulthood* (Coleman *et al.*, 1974) by and large makes a similar point of the dilemma of youth socialization in modern industrial or post-industrial society. Teichler (1976) has recently conducted a well-documented study in Japan. Since this is a country whose educational system operates under rather special historical and socio-cultural conditions, one should be careful not to generalize from it. But Teichler shows that the Japanese problems in a strikingly similar way have begun to beset Western European countries and can be conceived of as problems inherent in the pattern of industrial society.

Economist Kenneth Arrow once advanced the view that the educational system primarily serves as a 'filter' or certification device for the employment system and his colleague Lester Thurow (1972) has advanced a job competition model according to which job seekers are lined up according to their formal qualifications. Those who have amassed the highest number of years of schooling are first considered. Thus, job seekers compete according to credentials and not according to wage demands. The effect has been that first-degree holders are taking jobs that previously were occupied by secondary school graduates, who in their turn are pushing out those who are either drop-outs or have only completed elementary schooling.

Japan is a striking example of a modern industrial society with almost perfect 'fit' between formal education (obtained in a hierarchy of educational institutions of different prestige levels) and the availability of attractive jobs in civil service, business, and industry. Dore (1976) in his book *The Diploma Disease* has an excellent essay on Japan. Teichler (1976) has, as mentioned above, a well-documented study on the same 'dilemma of the modern industrial society' as it is felt at the university level. Each country has its particular hierarchy of prestige amongst institutions and amongst faculties and programmes within institutions. The common feature is that prestige level and competitive selectivity are highly, and sometimes almost perfectly, correlated. Another common feature is that each step in the formal system of general education tends increasingly to be perceived as a preparation for the next stage. No stage assumes a rounded-off profile of its own in terms of the competencies provided.

The excessive credentialism and preoccupation with school marks, examinations, and diplomas leads to distortions of basic educational values and to dysfunctions in the educational processes. The emphasis on examinations tends to lead to the neglect of the less tangible objectives that do not lend themselves as easily to measurement, such an initiative, perseverance, study skills, co-operative ability, ability to take responsibility, and the like. The content of the curriculum becomes secondary to the gaining of a diploma which breeds a trend towards 'curricular irrelevance'. Credentialism also leads to neglect of the specific competence needed in the occupational domain for which a particular course is supposed to prepare.

As pointed out above, increased competition leads to increased differentiation of prestige and ensuing benefits in terms of employment opportunities once the course has been completed. Therefore, many universities or faculties, by increasing their entrance requirements, can achieve increased prestige and attractiveness. In some countries where business schools in recent decades have become increasingly attractive, students with excellent marks tend to apply for admission simply because it is conceived as a 'waste' not to use their good credentials for entry to a programme with a high prestige leading to well-paid jobs. Whether the study and the career it leads to are compatible with the particular interest of the young person becomes a secondary matter.

Another serious problem is the 'new under-class' that is recruited from those who (often right from the beginning) are school failures, such as backward readers, grade repeaters, and drop-outs, many of whom are from underprivileged homes. They later represent the recruiting pool for the menial jobs as well as for socio-pathological phenomena, such as crime and drug abuse. Their situation becomes increasingly aggravated during their school attendance. In several big city secondary schools in Europe and North America about 30–35 per cent of all the 13–16-year-olds are simply not present in their classroom on a given day. They have 'voted with their feet'. The early leavers with low qualifications quit school with extremely negative attitudes and with low job expectations.

9

Reshaping the School for the Next Decades

THE present chapter does not pretend to advance a blueprint for a school reform. It is, however, on a more modest vein an attempt to advance measures geared to overcome or relieve the 'institutional malaise'. On the basis of our study in previous chapters of its aetiology, I shall venture to sketch changes in the institutional arrangements and educational practices called for in order to bring about both a closer connection between school and society and increased opportunities for individual self-realization.

My main concern is how the school as an institution relates to society at large. As has become apparent by the previous review of the criticisms levelled against the school, the relationship is subject to highly divergent interpretations depending upon the ideological spectacles through which the analyst is looking. One typical issue could serve as an illustration. Is the 'gap' between the school and working life, as described by the Panel on Youth, to be regarded as a 'real' one, or is it merely a temporary 'structural contradiction' that interferes with a basic correspondence between the social relations in the school and at the work place?

I submit that there are indications of a progressive institutionalization and bureaucratization of the school which are outcomes of centralization and institutional growth. In modern industrial society these processes are largely independent of the particular social order. I further submit that such a development is counter to genuine educational pursuits which have to occur in the small group setting with its needs of informality, flexibility, and enduring contacts, where the central task for the teacher is to organize learning opportunities for the individual student. The increased institutionalization has widened the gap between the school and society. Thus one overriding problem when it comes to 'reshaping', particularly at the secondary school level, is how to 'de-institutionalize' the school so as to bring about a better communication, a better integration with society at large, not least the world of work.

The rationale for supporting an institution such as the school is that it provides in a planned way vicarious instead of direct experience. Systematic learning that is prerequisite to the acquisition of competencies needed for self-realization and self-support in modern technological society cannot occur entirely in the informal setting of the family, the peer group, and the adult working groups. The process of upbringing and socialization, particularly in urban society, has become fragmented and inconsistent. The family, the pre-school institution, the peer groups in the playground, the school, voluntary associations such as the church and the hobby club, and, not least, the mass media, do not together constitute a systematic and/or integrated learning system. Even in totalitarian societies where ideological pluralism is rejected, one cannot dispense with an institution which is in charge of the planned transfer of certain basic skills but also of imparting systematic knowledge about the immediate and the remote environment in a world with a continuously widening horizon. The more the horizon opens up beyond the home, the village, and the region, the more important it becomes to convey experiences that young people are unlikely to gain by direct participation in adult life.

To the repertoire of basic literacy and numeracy skills should be added the mastering of abstract concepts needed in coping with science, administration, art, and literature. The development of these concepts requires systematic guidance on the part of a specialist in arranging learning opportunities, a professional person called a teacher.

On the basis of the studies and considerations in previous chapters I shall focus my observations in this chapter on three main issues:

(1) The relationship between school and work, dealing mainly with problems of transfer from school to working life, and with the repercussions of the social reward system on what goes on in the school.

(2) The governance and administration of the school in the 'learning society'.

(3) The 'inner life' of the school, both inside and outside the classroom.

A key issue that pervades all three problem areas is, as we have seen, the role of formal education in distributing status and preparing for occupational roles. This function in achievement-oriented, industrial societies with their emerging meritocratic patterns and demand for highly qualified manpower has gained rapidly in importance. The broadening of opportunities has brought in new groups of young people aspiring for the rewards that traditionally have been associated with further formal education. We are faced with the paradox that the more the educational system has expanded, the harder the competition for entry into its upper stages.

Hopes held for the school as the Great Equalizer did not materialize, either in the way or to the extent that had been envisioned. To be sure, the opening up of opportunities for all and the more uniform and fair provision of school facilities made it possible for a higher proportion of young people from lower social strata and remote areas to get access to further education. But concomitantly with the broadening of opportunities formal education has become an increasingly important criterion in selecting people for jobs and for job promotion. Young people are today keenly aware that their future depends mainly upon the formal credentials they have been able to amass in terms both of how much schooling they have absorbed and how well they have performed during their school years. The school has increasingly assumed the role of an institution for sorting and sifting. Instead of being the Great Equalizer it has become the Great Sorting Machine. It confers distinctions in terms of marks, examinations, certificates, and diplomas. It makes differences at school entry even wider as the young people progress through the system.

In all industrial nations the social pressures for equality of educational opportunity and the ensuing rise in expectations have, as O'Toole (1977) puts it, 'overheated the educational system, building expectations for higher social status that are not likely to abate'. (p. 59) More education breeds expectations about working conditions: the design and management of work and participation in decision-making at the work place. Particularly, young people expect jobs to be more challenging and self-fulfilling. There is, as has been shown by recent surveys, a tendency to value intrinsic rewards, such as self-fulfilling and meaningful jobs, more than money, status, and security. Young people shun repetitive, fragmented, and dull jobs with little scope for self-determination and autonomy.

I shall not elaborate here on why this development is taking place in spite of a strong meritocratic element inherent in advanced industrial and post-industrial societies. Educated talent has become a commodity in growing demand in highly industrialized societies, where technology in a wide sense and in all areas, manufacturing, services, communications, and—not least—education and research and development, is the prerequisite for high standards and economic growth. The meritocratic syndrome cuts across widely different social and economic orders. One therefore wonders if anything can be done in order to remove, or at least relieve, the competitiveness, selectivity, and scrambling for credentials that are part of the meritocratic syndrome or if such disadvantages are the price we have to pay for maintaining a high-standard technological society. It appears that as long as highly trained competence is necessary in order to maintain our technological culture and keep our complex society running, the corresponding competence will be singled out for particular rewards. But the socially differentiating effects could be kept under control by restructuring the relationship between education and work and—above all—by restructuring the world of work itself. I shall later in this chapter discuss certain policies that have been advanced in recent debates on education and work for the purpose of easing the transition from education to work—and vice versa.

Before embarking upon a discussion of the three issues mentioned earlier I shall briefly deal with the competencies the school should provide in modern society for those who are going to live in the rapidly changing society of today and tomorrow.

There are basically two sets of skills required: on one hand, certain cognitive skills traditionally imparted by the school at its best; and on the other, certain social skills, psychologically based in the affective domain, such as skills for relating to other persons, decision-making skills, and organizational skills which become increasingly important in a complex society with which the individual has to cope as an employee, customer, entrepreneur, and manager. The school as an institution can play only a very limited role in achieving the latter type of goals. Other agents, such as the family, community groups, and the work place, have to provide the main learning environments conducive to the development of social maturity.

The traditional school is usually well equipped to impart intellectual skills and basic knowledge. But in a changing society the school cannot provide an intellectual fare of specific items of knowledge for lifelong use. The shift that has to take place in the content of teaching is one from emphasis primarily on transmission of specific items of knowledge, which may soon become obsolete, to one with emphasis on intellectual skills that are applicable to a broad—and largely unforeseen—repertoire of tasks and situations. Priority has to be given to the ability to learn new things, that is to say, to skills conducive to independent study. Skills of particular importance are the ones instrumental in communication. Those who lack the ability to communicate adequately in their mother tongue tend in the long run to remain or fall below the poverty line. Decision-making power in complex situations and the ability to deal with bureaucratic organizations depend not only upon the mastering of the know-how about society, for instance, where and how to obtain information, but also on the ability to master the verbal and conceptual instruments which carry relevant messages.

The school of today should convey to its students an awareness that what they learn during their school years does not suffice for the rest of their active life. A school preparing for tomorrow would have to instil in its students the notion that education in our time is not something received and completed in childhood and adolescence but is a lifelong process. The dilemma, however, is that instead of getting a taste for more, a sizeable number of the students learn to dislike school. This is one reason, among several, why new opportunities opened up by programmes of adult education have not appealed to those who are socially deprived and who could have gained most from such programmes.

ESTABLISHING CONNECTIONS BETWEEN
SCHOOL AND WORK

In recent years the relationship between education and work
has become an issue of the highest priority because of the growing awareness of an institutional mismatch between them. We
are here dealing with a problem with far-reaching implications
for social and economic policy. Any discussion of how to
'integrate' schooling and work cannot avoid the central issue of
how the educational system relates to the employment system.
There are, as we have seen, completely opposing views on how
the two systems relate. On the one hand are those who maintain
that the educational system should 'prepare' for society and its
working life by and large as they are. Every person by means of
schooling should be given an equal opportunity to acquire the
competencies he wants in order to gain entry to the labour
market and to be employed thereafter according to his qualifications. On the other hand are those who maintain that the
educational system in a market economy serves to reproduce the
social relations in productive life, that is to say, serves to maintain the hierarchy between the owners of the means of production and wage earners.

Leaving aside the philosophical problem of how education
and working life relate, it is still possible to identify several basic
changes which have occurred in society at large and which
affect the relationship between education and work. The most
striking difference between what young people in the age range
14–18 do now and what they did a few decades ago is, of course,
that today nearly all of them are in school. Earlier only a social
and intellectual minority went on for further education; the
majority left school and entered the adult working society.

But the working life itself has also gone through far-reaching
changes. The most obvious changes are, of course, the shifts
from agriculture and manufacturing to service industry and the
disappearance of many unqualified jobs—even if many still
remain. Production has become more capital-intensive since
labour has become more expensive. This has strongly affected
the employment prospects of young people.

The relationship between education and work has begun to
be perceived in a more dynamic way. The difficulty for young

graduates in finding jobs that meet their expectations is usually referred to as a problem of 'over-education'. I agree with O'Toole that the expression is misleading and that the problem is essentially one of underemployment. It is a problem of making better use of the educated and of redesigning jobs so as to meet better the over-all educational qualifications of job seekers. 'Over-education', as conceived by many, will over the next decades be a chronic disease in the highly industrialized countries and cannot be remedied by limiting access to further schooling. A Joint Working Party of the OECD Committees on Education and on Manpower and Social Affairs as well as the Governing Board of the Centre for Educational Research and Development refer to this problem as the 'reciprocal adaptation of economics to individual abilities and desires' (OECD, 1977d, p. 12).

Highly rationalized and efficiency-oriented industry wants workers with a high level of job skills who on entry can perform efficiently in order for the company to maintain its competitive position. Therefore, school leavers who cannot achieve on a par with fully-fledged workers have difficulties in entering the 'first job' market. The structure of production has also changed so as to reduce the number of those who perform 'errand-boy' functions which earlier constituted a form of apprenticeship.

The growing realization of the lack of adequate connections between schooling and working life was one of the reasons why the OECD Council in 1973 asked the Secretary-General of the organization to set up an *ad hoc* committee of experts to prepare a policy paper, in which some major problems were brought into focus and recommendations made to achieve a better integration between education and the job world (OECD, 1975a). The lack of adequate connections is, as has been elaborated, due to changes that have taken place in the roles of the family, school, and work place. There has been a marked tendency to delegate more and more responsibilities to the schools, which have tended to become more isolated from society. There is a strong feeling that a solution is not to 'deschool' but to 'de-institutionalize' the school and to bring it into closer contact with society at large, including the other competence-producing agents. At the same time certain measures conducive to 're-schooling' the work place have to be contemplated.

The lack of connection between school and working life is not, however, primarily due to a failure of the school to provide 'saleable skills' but rather to an absence of real work orientation. This I have earlier referred to as a lack of 'functional participation'. Is it necessary for teenage students to spend the whole day being instructed by teachers who also spend the entire day on the same premises? Is it necessary to throw young people abruptly out into the labour market after the completion of a full package of education as defined by a set curriculum, often a uniform national one? One could consider a more gradual transition which step by step initiates young people into adult responsibilities. A major alternative is the one of a 'sandwiching' of classroom instruction and part-time work in enterprises outside the school, but not without contact with and supervision by the school. The so-called practical vocational guidance programme in Sweden is a work-experience programme which is taken for a few weeks by *all* students before completion of the nine-year mandatory school. It is part of a systematic vocational guidance programme designed to offer young people at least a taste of the conditions in the job world. Experience of the programme shows that the students following the work experience period return to school with enhanced motivation. It is as if school work had gained more relevance. These experiences apply to teenagers still of mandatory school age. In countries where the majority enters upper secondary school, one could give those who are in school from sixteen to eighteen an opportunity to acquire work experiences over a longer period, or spend part of the day in school and part of it at a work place.

Efforts to get students temporarily or permanently into the world of work are running up against the stumbling block represented by a highly rationalized and cost-effective economy. Youngsters coming directly from school—as well as workers close to retirement—are not considered profitable prospects by employers. Furthermore, as pointed out in the OECD (1975a) report, legislation about pay and the social responsibilities of employers can act as barriers to the hiring of young people. Instead, subsidies and tax incentives to employ young workers should be provided. For example, employers in some countries who hire young people under a certain age are eligible for state subsidies for the wages paid to these workers.

Our society is in certain respects an age-segregated one. Young people have little contact with adults in their daily occupations. Since retired people are taken care of in separate institutions or are provided with separate housing, the young have few, if any, contacts with the aged. But in order to mature they must have opportunities to meet the adult world in its various facets. If such encounters are to be a maturing experience, young people must have opportunities to work with adults in real-life situations. Teenage students could for certain periods practise in occupations in the rapidly expanding, labour-intensive public service sector, such as in child care, pre-school institutions, hospitals, and old-age care. Although their contributions might be modest, they could certainly be highly meaningful. It would give them experience of persons from other generations and social backgrounds and of how to relate to them. Not least, it would promote an aspect of social maturation which in our society tends to remain under-developed, namely to have other people dependent upon one's actions. Young people until the end of their teens are almost systematically indoctrinated into the role of being *clients*, of being dependent upon parents and teachers.

Older students could teach their younger schoolmates. Considering the tenacity of time-honoured educational practices and the resistance on the part of the teaching profession this would seem rather utopian; but experimental evidence gained so far is encouraging in terms of the benefits gained by those who are taught (for instance remedial reading), but also by those who teach.

Work experience also means working *with* other people, which implies that one gets involved in interdependent activities directed towards common goals. This is also something that the competition and scrambling for marks in school almost systematically prevents students from experiencing.

The difficulties in getting school leavers meaningful jobs have in recent years become aggravated. Whereas the unemployment rate among adult workers in the OECD countries has lately been in the range 2–9 per cent since the early 1970s among young people of 16 to 24 it has been in the 20–30 per cent range. The high rate of unemployment among early school leavers is perennial and relatively independent of the economic trends. The main reason for this is, as pointed out above, that employers want workers with a full productive capacity. This makes it difficult to employ young people without experience and previous on-the-job training. Lower secondary school leavers and drop-outs carry the worst burden and have the highest unemployment. There is a great difference in the unemployment rate between young people with upper secondary school diplomas or university degrees on the one hand and early school leavers on the other. Furthermore, the 'over-educated', much better than the 'under-educated', can achieve self-fulfilment in the world of work, because their broader outlook, allied with their higher level of skills, enables them more easily to redefine their jobs and thereby to achieve substitutability.

Transition from school to work can be facilitated by various integrative measures taken within the educational sub-system only. However, a labour market policy consistent with the aims of establishing integration would have to be formulated to support the steps taken within education.

Work–study programmes in some countries are already part of the secondary school curriculum with work experience provided in the enterprises. For instance, all students in grades 8 and 9 in Sweden are exposed to what is called 'practical vocational guidance' which involves visiting some enterprises in grade 8 and spending a couple of weeks at a place of work in grade 9. The Haby school reform in France which went into effect in 1977 envisages that some 10 per cent of the students' time will be devoted to 'external contacts'.

One suburban school district, Botkyrka, in the vicinity of Stockholm—a community which has been settled largely in the last decade and where many residents are immigrant workers—has applied to the National Board of Education for permission to conduct a pilot project. The 'book-weary' students, a euphemism for those who lack motivation to complete all the nine years of mandatory schooling, would be given an opportunity to take jobs at carefully selected work places under the supervision of the guidance personnel from their school. The supervisors are placed alongside the young people at the work place. A sense of meaningfulness would be provided by letting them take more responsibility and initiative than is usually possible in the highly structured and inflexible world of the school where so much is planned from the top downwards. The project is seen as a first step on the way to 'recurrent' education. The system is referred to as the 'adapted course of study'.

A system of sandwiching of the classroom and the work place is another provision that has been practised for many years in the Soviet Union and is part of the 'dual system' in the Federal Republic of Germany. An important step in the direction of de-institutionalization would be to let young people choose their learning experiences in the labour market, which would stimulate the establishment of attractive and productive learning places. This fits into the new concept of work-force planning spelled out by O'Toole (1977): 'Instead of trying to predict demand, train workers for specific tasks, and match them to jobs ... [we] can create a labor market that is fluid, flexible, and diverse, one characterized by change, greater freedom of choice, and a heavy accent on providing workers with the opportunity to achieve their own growth and learning needs—as *they* define them and at their own pace'. (p. 167)

Another step in the direction of providing work experience relates to the work mode practised in the school. Traditionally, classroom instruction has been of the frontal variety: the teacher turning to the entire class. Emphasis is placed on individual achievements and their assessment. The main obstacle in implementing the rhetoric about social education and group work has been the sorting and sifting role that the school increasingly has had to play. It has distortive effects also on the work–study and vocational programmes at the secondary level. The selection for university entry in countries with some kind of *numerus clausus* is casting its shadow over the upper secondary stage. One way of coming to grips with this is to diversify admission criteria and to let work experience carry enough weight to make practical programmes attractive. Such an arrangement can, however, have adverse effects on the 'academic core system' at the university, and the price in terms of intellectual excellence could be high.

On the whole, changes in both the material and psychological reward systems would have to be made in working life in order to achieve a better balance between the attraction of continued schooling compared to taking a job.

Education in the future can be envisioned as becoming the warp running through the life career pattern. The present lock-step system divides the life-cycle into one period of formal education which 'prepares' for the active working career, after which one retires. It is conducive to age segregation. It can be broken up by creating a system of 'recurrent' education which provides a flexibility of options and possibilities for career changes that can bring self-fulfilling jobs within the reach of individuals. It will facilitate transitions between the previously 'ghettoized' stages in life.

In the enthusiasm for 'career education' there has been an upsurge of vocational education based on the belief that young people are unemployed because they lack specific marketable skills needed for employment. The truth is that they lack a good general education on which to build such skills. The degree of substitutability increases with the level of formal education, which means that educational planning can be based on man-power projections to an even lesser extent than before. One is led to the paradoxical conclusion that the best vocational education is solid, high quality, general education.

The more hiring practices and selection of job seekers are based on formal credentials, the less important specific vocational schooling will become. There is a clear trend towards moving the transmission of specific vocational competencies to on-the-job training programmes.

In order to come to grips with the problem of youth unemployment, which is endemic in modern industrial societies with free market systems, certain legislative steps have to be taken. At present those who continue school beyond the mandatory age, say fifteen or sixteen, are given free tuition in most countries and in some cases means-tested allowances. The tuition costs alone in highly industrialized countries amount to some 3,000 U.S. dollars per student per year. Those who leave after having completed mandatory schooling, and who under the conditions described above run almost a 50 per cent risk of being unemployed for a considerable part of their time before the age of eighteen, should be entitled to the same public support as those who continue school. Equivalent support could take the form of subsidies to employers willing to provide work places with opportunities for continuous training and career development prospects.

Every young person who has completed mandatory schooling, in order to be saved from the ego-damaging frustration of being deprived of meaningful employment at an early age, should be *guaranteed* by law one of three alternatives:*

(1) A job which in most cases would have to be publicly subsidized either by direct grants or tax concessions. Supervision by public authorities should be required, at least until the age of 18. Voluntary, part-time school attendance for classroom instruction should be permitted.

(2) A place as an apprentice, by and large with the same provisions as under (1).

(3) A place in an upper secondary school, for which selection would have to occur.

By the same token legislation is needed to protect older workers from job displacement through the hiring of less costly, publicly subsidized younger workers. Such safeguards might be regarded by hard-line adherents of an unbridled, 'free' economy as 'socialist interference'. But they should rather be seen as structural support for the maintenance and preservation of the market system.

I have pointed out that the particular strength of the school in our society is that in a planned, systematic way it provides competencies and vicarious experiences which cannot be provided by other socializing agents. But the necessary, vicarious function easily becomes a serious limitation when schooling has become institutionalized to the extent that only certified teachers are allowed to teach. The tendency for the educational system to become a closed society on its own is further strengthened by the way teachers are trained. Young people who want to become teachers go directly from secondary schools to teacher training institutions. After their certification they then begin to teach in school. The lack of experience of work outside the pedagogical

* After completion of the manuscript I have found that this is by and large the same policy as that recommended by a Joint Working Party set up by various OECD organs (OECD, 1977d).

sphere is a handicap for a teacher conveying notions about the world outside the school. It is, therefore, of the utmost importance to provide prospective teachers with work experience prior to their entering teacher training.

Another step towards alleviating the drawbacks of institutional isolation is to draw upon expertise from outside the school, persons representing various sectors of the working life, but also those who are experienced in public affairs. Every competent holder of an occupation is a potential pedagogue, since he possesses some important experience and competence which can be transferred to the next generation. Outside experts used to supplementing the efforts of certified teachers would also help to alleviate the ritualistic features of instruction that easily develop, when the emphasis on examinations, marks, and diplomas tends to push concern with the content of the curriculum into the background.

EDUCATION AS A 'HOLDING OPERATION'

A considerable proportion of secondary school students in the age range 13–16 have extremely negative attitudes towards schooling. Many would have preferred to drop out of school had not two restraints prevented it. In the first place, they are forced by law to stay on until the end of mandatory school age. Yet an increasing number of youngsters simply do not turn up. In some big city school districts as many as 25–35 per cent are absent from school on any given day. In the second place, those who turn up most of the time are keenly aware that they have to 'stick it out' in order to become eligible for the more attractive jobs. A majority of the young people who say that they do not like school nevertheless proceed 'voluntarily' to upper secondary school in countries such as the United States, Sweden, or the Netherlands (Husén *et al.*, 1973). They stay on in spite of the ritualistic, qualification-earning, boring, and anxiety-creating instruction to which many of them are subjected.

Publicly supported education has increasingly become a 'holding operation' from the point of view of both the individual and society. The experts invited by OECD to give their views on educational policies and trends in the Member Countries point out: 'Until economic and manpower policies succeed in reinstating full employment the education system may have to face an increased demand from some of those who would otherwise have left school and joined the labour force.' (OECD, 1977b, p. 19) High youth unemployment has become endemic, with a rate of 50 per cent among those who have achieved only the legal minimum of formal education. Education beyond the mandatory minimum gives the individual two advantages. It postpones his entry into an uncertain unemployment-ridden labour market and enhances his possibilities of becoming employed later, since the amount of formal schooling tends to be used by employers as the first selection criterion for choosing among job seekers. Furthermore, additional formal education helps the individual to redefine his employability and makes him eligible for a wider range of jobs.

But a 'holding operation' means a heavy drain on public resources, even if one considers the alternative, namely, the costs incurred by the national economy in support of unemployed youth. It is, of course, a more serious economic problem than open unemployment in countries with limited resources, which is the case in the Third World. Education is a labour-intensive industry that draws heavily on public resources. Using schooling as a device for reducing unemployment represents a diversion of resources that could otherwise have been used to create new job opportunities.

What should be carefully considered from an educative as well as from a financial point of view is the cost of a 'holding operation' where youngsters, many of whom are not very motivated, are kept in school year after year, compared to the costs of a system where they are gradually placed in jobs which for some time have to be subsidized at public expense. Work in enterprises supervised by the school, combined with some classroom teaching, may not be less educative than going to school full-time. Job experience is educative in terms of establishing the social maturity and the competence needed in order to get along in society. The indications that this alternative would prove less costly are strong.

GOVERNANCE AND ADMINISTRATION

The objectives of school education are usually stated in official documents: laws enacted by parliaments, decrees issued by central party committees, ministerial ordinances, and pre-ambles to curricula. In such documents the objectives are presented at an extremely general—and abstract—level far removed from the concrete classroom behaviours into which, by successive operations, they might be broken down. Consensus can easily be reached about generalizations that contain noble phrases to which everybody is willing to pay lip-service. The gap between the rhetoric of the official documents and the realities of the classroom is perceived by teachers and others who have to carry the practical burden to be quite striking, not to say frustrating. Teachers talk about the curricular 'poetry' in contrast with the hardships and tribulations of the tangible classroom realities.

As the educational system grows, the educational bureaucracy, at both the central and local levels, becomes more powerful. In recent years, the two issues of size and centralization–decentralization have become more acute. After a long period of consolidation, when schools and school districts were merged, governance of schools has come into fewer and fewer hands. For instance, in Sweden the number of municipalities has been consolidated from about 3,000 to 300 which has led to a considerable attenuation of grassroots contacts with governing and administrative bodies. At the same time the school units, particularly at the secondary level, have become larger and larger.

Naturally, the concern has been with the negative aspects of size. Formalism, bureaucratic rigidity, lack of social control and of personal contacts in the big organizations, lead to problems of personal identity and discipline. But there is an obvious trade-off here. Richness of provisions with regard, for instance, to curriculum and laboratories, as well as ease of access to certain pedagogical, social, and medical services, require a certain minimum size. The advantages of economies of size have to be weighed against the psychological advantages of smallness.

On the Western European scene, for example, there are wide differences in the degree of centralization–decentralization in school administration. Some countries, such as Sweden and France, have centralized systems to the extent that even the curriculum is set at the national level and a major portion of the operational costs for schools are allocated by the central government. Countries like England and the Netherlands, in contrast, have rather decentralized systems. There is, of course, no universal yardstick that can be employed in deciding how much centralization or decentralization is 'just right'. As in the case of size there is a trade-off between them, and the optimal 'solution' varies from country to country. Of cardinal importance here is the amount of participation on the part of parents, teachers, and students in school-site decision-making.

School reforms that affect the structure of the system and have consequences for logistics, such as buildings and equipment, can be more easily implemented by national legislation. The shifting political majorities of various *Länder* in the Federal Republic of Germany have led to stagnation in efforts to change the structure and the over-all provision for education (Becker *et al.*, 1976). The problem can somewhat paradoxically be stated like this: the framework for decentralization and local autonomy sometimes calls for central control which then serves as a safeguard against the excesses of local interest groups *vis-à-vis*, for instance, minorities. The wide disparities in financial resources that have been, and to some extent still are, so glaring in the United States are consequences of local autonomy which leads to decisions that bring about wide inequalities in educational provision.

The quest for accountability and evaluation of what the school achieves with the resources that taxpayers put at its disposal has strong political overtones, since in addition to the use of resources it also concerns the standards attained by the students.

Participatory democracy in the school has in addition to its inherent political values certain pedagogical ones. Involvement of the students in the decision-making and management of the schools contributes to the achievement of objectives such as co-operation, responsibility, and initiative.

As was pointed out in Chapter 7, education is in a sense 'ungovernable'. Governance of the conventional type is conducted under the assumption of predictability and detailed planning of steps taken according to formal rules. But the educative process is, by being interactive, inherently unpredictable, or is in any case beset with a wide margin of uncertainty.

THE 'INNER LIFE' OF THE SCHOOL

The 'bureaucratic' and formalistic setting which makes changes so difficult to achieve, even those to which all parties involved pay lip-service, was dealt with at some length at the second Aspen–Berlin international seminar on the Future of Schooling. The major points made are summed up here.

Observers of what is happening in the classroom who compared experiences made over a long time-span, and in some cases across national boundaries, came out with three conclusions:

(1) Educational practices show a remarkable tenacity or persistence against even highly valued efforts to change. It was pointed out by Philip Jackson at a Berlin seminar that the United States, for example, has over the last fifteen years 'lived through a spirit of reform that did not materialize'. Similar experiences were reported from other countries.

(2) Educational practices seem to show a high degree of incorrigibility. Are the changes noticed in these practices just cyclical? Prescribed changes tend to be submerged by mainstream practices. The same seems to apply to spontaneous 'faddish' innovations.

(3) Educational practices tend to show a high degree of 'contextual relativity' which seems to confirm Dilthey's view that there are few, if any, pedagogical principles that transcend cultures. Are there any on-the-whole universally valid pedagogical principles?

The drawbacks of the big school particularly affect the contacts between the teacher and the individual student which take place in an impersonal and formal atmosphere. The larger the enrolment, the more difficult the social control in the school. The central task for the teacher is to arrange learning opportunities for the individual student, not only for the class as a whole. In order to achieve this, provisions have to be made for informal, flexible, and continuing contacts. In the big school human relations by necessity tend to be more formal and rigid. Disruptions in contacts are more frequent between teachers and students. Social control in a wide sense requires 'watching eyes' in a small group setting with individual visibility and frequent personal and informal contacts. An enrolment exceeding 400–500 students makes it difficult for the principal and the teachers to identify the students who belong to the school. When it rises to 1,000–1,500, difficulties in even identifying the teacher begin to be felt.

As pointed out above, there is an obvious trade-off between the bureaucratic rigidity of the big school with broad and specialized offerings and the informal contacts in the small school with narrow offerings. One solution that is found in British private secondary schools is to divide the school into 'houses' which are administratively semi-independent and, in interpersonal contacts, almost entirely independent. Thereby, the social contacts between teachers and students, as well as within the student body, can be enhanced. In schools enrolling the entire age range of mandatory schooling where students in the early grades easily fall victims to harassment on the part of their older school-mates, separate school yards can reduce the nuisance.

Differentiation of formal schooling into stages and types of schools is quite old. But the practice of organizing a school in 'grades' or 'forms' is much more recent. When schools were small, often consisting of only one classroom, students of varying ages and competencies had to be taught together. This necessitated pedagogical practices such as independent work, individualization, and tutoring by more advanced classmates, techniques which in recent times have been rediscovered as 'progressive' and conducive to valuable educational goals.

Traditional classroom teaching seems to die hard. The experiences presented at international seminars conducted for the Aspen project consistently point to the 'tenacity' and 'incorrigibility' of teaching practices. Somebody even raised the question whether they could be substantially changed at all. Frontal instruction prevails in spite of all the efforts made in teacher training to introduce more 'progressive' and individualized methods aimed at promoting objectives such as independence, individual initiative, responsibility, and co-operation. The contention that drastic reduction of class size would promote more individualized modes of work does not seem to hold, since massive empirical evidence shows that both work modes and outcomes in terms of pupil competence seem to be largely un-related to class size within the 20-35 range.

Seminar participants expressed concern about erosion of the quality of instruction in many schools. All too frequently the observer finds classroom instruction dull, unimaginative, and badly presented. As a means of improving instructional quality it was recommended that some acceptable means of monitoring instruction be devised, particularly at the secondary level.

THE ROLE OF THE TEACHER AND TEACHER EDUCATION

A teacher can be defined as an organizer of learning opportuni-ties for the individual student. His task is a continuous and systematic one requiring him to guide the learning process itself and check the outcomes. The balance between these three tasks determines the teacher's role. In an achievement-oriented milieu the emphasis tends to be on his function as an examiner to the detriment of the other two. He easily combines his role as an examiner with the one of being a frontal transmitter of knowledge.

But in addition to the more 'technical' tasks the teacher also serves as a kind of model—under favourable circumstances as the friend to whom the children look up and whom they want to emulate. The dilemma is, however, that the role which the teacher has been assigned by society, that of a judge and a gate-keeper who determines success or failure in life, hardly squares with the one of being an understanding guide and friend. The teacher role of today, particularly at the secondary level where élite education within the span of a few decades has been re-placed by mass education, is beset with several dilemmas amongst which the one just mentioned is prominent.

The demands put on teachers in terms of the objectives they are expected to achieve are sometimes terrifying. They are traditionally supposed to transmit certain cognitive com-petencies. But the repertoire of tasks has been considerably widened by including a series of affective objectives, such as aesthetic taste, moral values, responsibility, initiative, and co-operation. The goals have been expanded without due regard to the means and resources for implementing them. The teachers often feel left in the lurch. They are frustrated by the discrepancy between the curricular 'poetry' and the resources needed to meet the expectations.

An oral report was presented at the second Aspen–Berlin seminar by Professor von Hentig dealing with educational innovations at the laboratory schools in Bielefeld, the Federal Republic of Germany, where the university has been closely involved in experimental education. The schools were almost completely 'left free' and were invited to prepare their own plans for experimental activities. A pattern of resistance to change developed, very similar to the one reported by Pusey (1976) in his study of school reform in Tasmania. The unwillingness to visit the classrooms of colleagues in the same school, let alone to visit classrooms in other schools, was part of this resistance. Job security also entered into the picture and fortified resistance, since it was backed by the unions. Specialized teachers often held a *Beamten* (civil servant) mentality which implied acceptance of a more formal and limited conception of their role as teachers.

'DE-INSTITUTIONALIZING' EDUCATION

We are said to live in a 'learning society', an expression that denotes certain salient properties of the learning milieu of our time. It is a society with rapidly changing material conditions, social relations, and values. The individual continually has to improve his competencies in order to be able to cope better with the changing conditions and requirements pertaining to his roles both as the holder of an occupation and as a citizen participating in the democratic process. But by improving his competencies and enhancing his coping power he also contributes to reshaping his milieu in order to make it fit better his changing values and aspirations. The impact of considerably extended formal schooling on attitudes toward working conditions and decision-making at the work place illustrates how education can actively contribute to bringing about societal changes (O'Toole, 1977; Levin, 1977).

'Lifelong' or 'recurrent' education is both effect and cause of a changing society. Competencies needed for full participation in working and social life are, in a static and ascriptive society, acquired almost entirely before entry to adult responsibilities. The individual is supposed to draw upon what he learned in childhood and early youth for the rest of his life. In a time of rapid technological and social change, however, we can seldom predict the *specific* competencies needed a few decades, or even a few years, hence. The need to learn and re-learn certain vocational skills is obvious. The changing social life and the opening up of new vistas, not least by the media, call for the acquisition of concepts and 'cognitive maps' that can help us to orient ourselves under new conditions. Consider, for example, the intensive debate that has followed in the wake of the energy crisis and the research on nuclear energy. The use of various sources of energy and their impact on the environment has implications that make it necessary for the majority of citizens to acquire rudimentary notions about the scientific and technological bases of energy generation and distribution, and their ecological and social impacts. The implication for formal schooling is that its emphasis should be on skills and concepts that are applicable to a broad and largely unforeseen range of situations.

The last few decades have seen a tremendous expansion of what in a wide sense could be called 'adult education', since the participants are adults, most of them with a substantial amount of work experience. Adult education in Europe was for a long time conducted under the auspices of popular movements, such as the labour and temperance movements. Its objective was to provide the disadvantaged with the general education they could not obtain in the regular school system since they had only had access to an often rather poor primary education. Secondary schools were for a social (and to some extent intellectual) élite who could afford it and who needed preparation for their class-determined role.

Another important objective of early adult education was to educate the leaders of the popular movement, for instance in the labour unions. When the idea, or rather the strategy, of 'recurrent' education gained momentum in educational debate and planning in some Western European countries around 1970 it was also conceived as a convenient means of providing vocational competencies and marketable skills by offering access to training courses as the need for new competencies emerged. But since the margin of uncertainty about the working life of the future and its specific requirements is large, programmes of recurrent education will have to serve a broader range of objectives. Thus general education is the best vocational preparation through its provision of a basic repertoire of skills and concepts. This has been the ideal of the adult education movement in some countries. Education in the study circles or evening classes of the workers' movement was not aimed at providing marketable skills or helping to achieve a better career, but was a means of self-realization and of enhancing the individual's capacity to serve the movement (Paulston, 1976).

The attainment of a more humanistic ideal of education requires changes in the reward system. This refers both to material and psychological rewards. I have repeatedly pointed out the meritocratic element inherent in modern industrial society. The demand for trained technological and managerial manpower has made education, and particularly formal education — thanks to the ease with which it can be used to sort people—a vehicle of social promotion and an elevator to higher wages and salaries. The broadening of opportunities in terms of the number of places available at upper secondary and tertiary institutions and the inclusion of young people from lower social strata in these institutions has intensified the competition for promotion in the system. In some countries the individual return on an investment in education has recently tended to decline (see, e.g., Freeman, 1976). But the psychological rewards tend to become relatively more important as the wage or salary floor is raised for the great mass of workers. The changing attitudes to education and work associated with the shift from instrumental to more expressive values might signal the advent of a societal climate with a less meritocratic flavour than the one that has prevailed so far, even in an economic system which values continued economic growth and raised standards of living.

WHAT FUTURE CAN BE ENVISAGED FOR THE SCHOOL AS AN INSTITUTION?

The project on institutional schooling, its 'crisis' symptoms, salient trends, and their determinants, is primarily not a futuristic exercise. However, in proposing measures to be taken in order to resolve the problems besetting today's school the future envisaged for it is by implication also spelled out. In addition to the views advanced at the Aspen seminars, I could draw upon interviews with half a dozen colleagues at the Graduate Schools of Education at Stanford University and at the University of Chicago. The outcomes of the seminars and the interviews are summed up under three main headings:

(1) Bureaucratization and centralization versus participatory democracy in education.

(2) Integration of education and working life.

(3) Unity versus diversity in educational provisions.

(1) *Bureaucratization and Centralization Versus Participation*

Those who believe that the centralized uniformity of a bureaucratic system of administration will rapidly and automatically bring about more equality in education are in for a disappointment. In a uniform system there are always some who are 'more equal than others'—and who know how to take advantage of it. Some are born with genetic and/or social advantages and, in drawing upon uniform provisions, thereby continue to enjoy advantaged positions. This has been evidenced in socialist and capitalist economies alike. Education is a process of interaction between teacher and learner that has a wide margin of indeterminacy. It therefore tends to be allergic to bureaucratic governance.

However, the other extreme, completely independent schools operating in a spirit of *laissez-faire*, does not solve the problem of equity in education either. On the contrary, it would even more enhance the advantages of those who start out privileged.

There is no universal 'proper balance' between centralized uniformity and decentralized diversity. The problem has been dealt with differently in various national systems of education depending upon special historical, social, and ethnic conditions.

Dramatically increased enrolment at the secondary and tertiary levels, soaring educational costs, and the mounting importance of education for an individual's life chances have brought the national government as an active partner into the educational scene, even in countries with a federal structure, where the states and local communities by constitutional right are entitled to autonomy in education. This has led to increased central control of how funds are used, with on the whole more emphasis on accountability.

An overriding question is: will the process of centralization and the building of central bureaucratic empires continue? Further, can this process be reversed—and by what policy actions? How can hierarchical decision-making be counteracted by increased grassroots-dominated participatory democracy? What kind of conflicts can be envisaged for years to come between bureaucratic and centralized administration on one hand and participatory democracy on the other?

Evidently, centralization and the concomitant bureaucratization are associated with demographic factors and with cost–benefit considerations which are pervasive in modern society and which also affect service-producing institutions. Rapid urbanization is conducive, of course, to the consolidation of school units and to centralization; otherwise the delivery system provided by the school cannot live up to public expectations. A certain minimum enrolment must be achieved, particularly at the secondary level, in order to serve the public adequately.

Centralization has, however, bred reverse tendencies carried by the quest for grassroots participation. Big metropolitan school systems in the United States have been divided into districts with separate superintendents covering smaller areas. Since the mid-1960s the quest for 'local control' has become more vociferous. The growing awareness of ethnic, language, and sex discrimination has had an impact. Since central governance and administration reduces heterogeneity and pluralism, decentralization promotes educational practices that better meet the needs of sub-groups. The voucher system also works against centralization through the leeway it gives parents in choosing the school they want for their children. Pilot projects have been launched in some places, where publicly supported mini-schools have been set up among which the parents can choose. The schools that attract more students receive more resources and vice versa. The so-called SIA-reform in Sweden (SOU, 1974) is an attempt to decentralize by setting up bodies at the local school level with certain decision-making powers. The same motive lies behind the provision of central grants to the local boards to be used with a wide margin of discretion.

The participation problem is closely related to the problem of bigness and central control. The possibilities of splitting the big units in an urban society are slight; the tendency of centralized bigness can hardly be reversed. The problem then becomes how to build in the advantages of smallness within the larger framework. In the final analysis this is a psychological problem: how to increase the sense of individual identity and participation. The problem is to arrange the large institutions so that teachers and students can relate to each other in smaller groups.

Participation in school affairs on the part of the local community varies considerably in mode and intensity among countries. On the whole the rather intense parent participation in the United States has no counterpart in Europe, whereas student participation in some European countries is more intense than in the United States. Since the school has increasingly become an arena of political conflicts—illustrations are the marking and examination system and university admission in some European countries, or integration in the United States— parental participation has increasingly been met by teacher resistance. In the wake of the accusation that schools do not perform what they are supposed to, for instance fail to teach the basic skills properly, the dilemma of amateurism versus professionalism has crept up. In such a situation it is extremely important that 'the noise is co-opted', that is to say, that lay opinion is engaged with professional opinion in a constructive dialogue.

(2) *Integration of Education and Working Life*

How do we bring salient changes in the outside world, not least in the world of work, to bear on what is happening in the school? This overriding question can be broken down into the following questions. How do we facilitate the transition from secondary school to work by including work experience in the curriculum? How do we bring competence outside the school to bear on instruction? What is the educational impact of industrial democracy? These problems have earlier been dealt with at some length and I thus limit myself to reference to the presentation above.

(3) *Unity Versus Diversity in Educational Provisions*

Unity and diversity of provisions refer to both content and administrative provision of education. For instance in the United States the ethnic wave to which Congress is very sensitive has been conducive to diversification in content. Requests have been made for subdivisions within school for programmes geared to the needs of various ethnic groups. But since 'mainstream' education tends to benefit those who under the prevailing societal conditions are most successful, there has been criticism against the ethnicity movement accusing it of putting the minorities in an unfavourable position with regard to their life chances. The allocation of children of ethnic minorities to programmes that 'we' think are best for them has a striking resemblance to the tracking of children with regard to academic ability at an early age.

The quest for accountability has influenced the amount of diversification that in reality, if not formally, is permitted. The National Assessment launched in the United States in the late 1960s could not but affect the schools in a unifying direction. The standard tests, introduced in 1944 in compulsory education in Sweden, have in all likelihood had a highly unifying effect. One study at the 14-year-old level showed the between-school variance as only 8 per cent of the between-student variance in Sweden as compared to more than 20 per cent in England and the United States (Peaker, 1975).

SOME ASSERTIONS ABOUT THE FUTURE

As a result of my attempts to assess the present problems of institutional schooling and to take bearings of the directions in which it seems to move, I would make the following assertions about education by the end of this century.

(1) Formal, full-time schooling of the traditional type will be somewhat reduced both in terms of the number of years of attendance and the amount of classroom instruction. Pre-school institutions will provide education for almost all children of the age range 4–6. Formal classroom instruction will go on from 6 until the age of about fifteen. Every young person will then have 'drawing rights' to another 4–6 years of education in institutions of his own choosing.

(2) A system of 'lifelong' or 'recurrent' education closely related to career-patterns and career-changes and with a wide range of individual options will be available. A gradual shift in priorities and in the allocation of expenditures to this system from the traditional system of schools for children and adolescents will take place.

(3) As a result of a change in values from 'instrumental' to 'expressive', important changes in the reward system both within and outside the educational system will also take place. Less emphasis will be placed on marks, diplomas, and certificates. The salary differentials for most jobs will not be related to the amount of formal education to the same extent as today.

(4) As a consequence of the strategy of 'recurrent' education and the introduction prior to school leaving of programmes of work experience and remedial programmes, transition from school to working life will be facilitated.

(5) Every school leaver will have the guaranteed option of a job, an apprenticeship position, or a place in further education.

(6) Increased participation by parents and students in decision-making related to smaller units within the big units, particularly at the secondary level, can be anticipated. The schools will increasingly become 'learning centres' serving all generations with a broad variety of programmes.

(7) The continued rising level of general education among workers in industry and business will enhance aspirations for participation in decision-making with regard to the management, the design of the production-process, and the work milieu.

(8) The effects of the explosion of specialized knowledge will generate a need for 'generalists': highly competent individuals with a broad interdisciplinary perspective and with the ability to think across specialities in trying to solve social and technological problems. They could be envisaged as becoming the 'meritocrats' of the twenty-first century.

CONCLUDING AND SUMMARY OBSERVATIONS

In the 1960s formal education was, virtually without reservation, seen as beneficial to both the individual and society. In the 1970s, however, this unquestioning support for and firm confidence in schooling gave way to disenchantment and severe criticism. In some quarters the word 'crisis' has been used to characterize the troubles besetting formal education, that is, institutional schooling. The change in public mood is reflected in the fact that educational issues have moved down the political—as well as the financial—priority scale. The establishment of 'alternative' or 'free' schools is but one of the symptoms of disenchantment.

The study reported in this book of the school as an institution in the highly industrialized societies has had a threefold purpose:

(1) to identify the symptoms of 'institutional malaise' that on both sides of the Atlantic beset particularly secondary education;

(2) to diagnose the causes of the malaise; and

(3) to contemplate institutional changes that could remedy the situation.

The approach has mainly been an analytical one; hence the emphasis has been put on the first two aims.

Overriding Issues

Our attempts to 'diagnose' the troubles that beset formal schooling in modern society have identified problems that cluster around four overriding issues:

(1) *Institutional isolation* of the school has deepened over the last few decades. For various reasons, such as broadened objectives, prolonged stay in school, bureaucratization, unionization, and consolidation of school districts, the school has become increasingly separated from society at large. This has, among other things, led to difficulties in the transition from schooling to work.

The marked change in the 'ecology' of education, with a rapid increase in the number of working mothers and increased exposure of children to television, has led to a widening of the responsibility of the school. It has taken over tasks that it is inherently ill-equipped to perform.

(2) There is an *equality-versus-meritocracy dilemma* that looms large in highly complex, technological societies. Behind the disenchantment with school among young people lie the difficulties of pursuing genuine educative values conducive to

self-fulfilment. In an era of massive rhetoric about equality of opportunity and broadened educational provision, advanced formal schooling is no longer the royal road to more attractive jobs and higher social status. This increasingly leads to frustrated aspirations.

The dilemma is this. On the one hand, the school provides competencies that in modern society increasingly constitute an individual power base. On the other hand, a marked streak of egalitarianism runs through the polity and has in most societies led to considerable increase of formal equality of opportunity— but not to increased equality of outcomes or results. The 'revolution of rising expectations' has led to a rapidly increased demand for advanced education. The marked imbalance between the number of graduates and the number of jobs traditionally available to them is noticeable in most highly industrialized societies. This has reinforced tendencies of credentialism in the world of work which in its turn has reinforced competition in the educational system. Formal qualifications increasingly determine the place the individual occupies in the line of job-seekers.

Since, from the outset, 'some are more equal than others', for instance have better educated parents, we find in both socialist and capitalist countries striking social class differences in participation in advanced education, in spite of universalization of secondary and massification of tertiary education. A result of the increased competition tends to be an emerging new underclass of young people from underprivileged families who have not been able to assert themselves in the competitive system.

(3) The *proper tasks or goals* of the school in modern society need to be better defined. As pointed out above, the school is ill-equipped to perform certain educative tasks assigned to it. In some instances the goals are in conflict with each other, such as education for co-operation in a highly competitive climate. But the most urgent priority is to define the tasks that the school is supposed to perform in relation to other educative institutions, such as family, media, libraries, religious organizations, etc. A more clear-cut differentiation of tasks is called for.

(4) Rising youth unemployment and increased institutional isolation of the school bring to the fore the need for *integrating education and the world of work*. This requires, in the first place,

changes in the conception of both. Work has to be conceived in a more dynamic way with a broader spectrum of options with regard to working time and relationship to education. 'Recurrent' education is beginning to be viewed as a strategy to achieve both greater equality and self-fulfilment, and greater flexibility between education and work.

More Specific Issues

A wide range of more specific issues leading to policy recommendations can be derived from the overriding ones quoted above which have served as an agenda for seminar discussions on both sides of the Atlantic. Needless to point out, no clear-cut policy actions will follow from the analyses conducted in the various chapters of the present book, not even for policy-makers who are in complete agreement with the outcomes of the analyses. The reason is, of course, that policy actions are always guided by factual information combined with values held by the policy-maker.

The purpose of the exercise reported in this book, including the seminars and workshops, has been to heighten the awareness among the participants of the roots of the problems and to widen their perspective so as to take in aspects of the problems that might otherwise have been left out. We have therefore found it more appropriate to formulate the specific issues (to which policy-makers should address themselves) as questions, instead of advancing sweeping recommendations.

(1) How do we *differentiate the educational purposes of the school* from the ones of the family, the media, the organizations, and the work place? How can we clarify the limits to what the school can undertake?

(2) How do we *adapt institutional structures to achieve realistic educational objectives* at the upper secondary level? More specifically, what is the most appropriate institutional setting for the education of young people in the age range fifteen to twenty? Can we conceive of a network of 'learning centres' with activities going on in schools, factories, apprenticeship places, etc? What kind of adjustments would have to be made both by formal institutions and workplaces? How do we in our society *gradually initiate young people into the adult world*, where they now

seem to be redundant? How can sandwiching between class-room and workplace best be organized? How much weight should be attached to work experience in admission to further education at the upper secondary and tertiary levels?

(3) At what age level should the inevitable *selection for élite education* take place? How do we arrange for 'second-chance' entry to furthergoing education in systems which at an early stage are selective?

(4) How do we establish at the secondary level a system of *plurality of excellence*, that is to say, a variety of career paths in formal schooling leading to different types of high-level competence other than academic ability? What changes in the reward system outside the educational sector are called for in order to achieve this and to alleviate the mounting credentialism?

(5) What changes are required in order to *cope with the dwindling financing of education*? How do we reallocate the resources between the various levels of education? Can the length of formal schooling be shortened to facilitate a better integration of education and work and, at the same time, incur less costs?

(6) How do we equip the educational system for *self-evaluation and self-renewal* in an era of growing bureaucracy? What kind of feedback mechanisms can be built into the system? How can rigidifying forces in the administration and the teaching force be overcome? How can educational research and development become an instrument for renewal?

(7) How do we *reshape governance and administration* of the educational system in order better to achieve the genuinely educational goals? How do models of participatory democracy (participation on the part of teachers, parents, and students) apply here?

(8) How can *pluralism in educational provision* be maintained so as to offer real options to the parents? How can we let the parents/consumers have 'access to a market' in order to implement the right to have options?

Having worked with planners and policy-makers at both national and international levels, I am keenly aware of how meaningless it is to try to come up with sweeping recommendations compiled in the laundry-list fashion. Such recommendations are particularly useless if they are not consistently related to the diagnosis conducted and to each other. They are, if they are taken seriously, dangerous, since piecemeal and short-term panaceas tend to be attractive to politicians given the conditions of office under which they operate. What we have in mind here, however, is a systems and long-range approach which, within the given societal setting, aims at reshaping the school as an institution in its entirety. Education does not operate in a social vacuum. Educational reforms cannot substitute for social reforms. The former must be part of the latter if they are going to have a lasting impact.

List of Participants

Participants in seminars and workshops sponsored by the Aspen Institute in connection with the project on institutional schooling.

Hellmut Becker
Hans Karl Behrend
Alain Bienaymé
Halcyon Bohen
George Bonham
Ernest L. Boyer
Jeffrey W. Bulcock
Lord Alan Bullock
Theodore W. Calhoun
Arye Carmon
Philip H. Coombs
Jonathan Croall
Marion Countess Doenhoff
Klaus von Dohnanyi
Dorothea Gaudart
Bertrand Girod de l'Ain
Ernst Goldschmidt
James Guthrie
Michael Haltzel
David Harman
Hartmut von Hentig
Philip W. Jackson
H. Thomas James
Henri Janne
Denis Kallen
Martin Kaplan
Francis Keppel
Bijan Khorram
Walter Kirz
Pieter de Koning

Stefan Kwiatkowski
Henry M. Levin
Milbrey McLaughlin
Stuart Maclure
Martin Meyerson
Hermann Minz
Alfonso Ocampo-Londono
Wincenty Okon
Rudy Oswald
G. S. Papadopoulos
Anthony Pascal
James A. Perkins
Sir Walter Perry
Hans-Henning Pistor
Lois Rice
W. Kenneth Richmond
Terry N. Saario
Uwe Schlicht
Hanna-Beate Schöpp-Schilling
James Sheffield
Rouhangise Sohrab
Shepard Stone
Jan Szczepanski
Mohammad Taher-Moayari
Gholamali Tavassoli
Ulrich Teichler
Michael Timpane
Eberhard Umbach
Lord John Vaizey
Aldo Visalberghi

References

ANASTASI, ANNE (1958) 'Heredity, Environment, and the Question "How?" ', *Psychological Review* **65**, 197–208.

ANDERSSON, BENGT-ERIK (1969) *Studies in Adolescent Behaviour*, Stockholm: Almqvist and Wiksell International.

BAILEY, STEPHEN (1976) *The Purposes of Education*, Bloomington, Indiana: Phi Delta Kappa.

BECKER, HELLMUT *et al.* (1976) *Die Bildungsreform—eine Bilanz*, Stuttgart: Klett.

BEHN, WILLIAM H., MARTIN CARNOY, WILLIAM A. CARTER, JOYCE C. CRAIN, and HENRY M. LEVIN (1974) 'School Is Bad; Work Is Worse', *School Review* **82**:1, 49–68.

BELL, DANIEL (1973) *Coming of Post-Industrial Society: A Venture in Social Forecasting*, New York: Basic Books.

BELL, DANIEL (1975) 'A "Just" Equality', *Dialogue* **8**:2, 85–8.

BERDIE, RALPH *et al.* (1962) *Who Goes to College? Comparisons of Minnesota Freshmen 1930–1960*, Minneapolis: University of Minnesota.

BEREDAY, GEORGE Z. F. (ed.) (1969) *Essays on World Education: The Crisis of Supply and Demand*, New York: Oxford University Press.

BEREITER, CARL (1973) *Must We Educate?*, Englewood Cliffs, N.J.: Prentice-Hall.

BERELSON, BERNARD (ed.) (1974) *Population Policy in Developed Countries*, New York: McGraw-Hill.

BERG, IVAR (1971) *Education and Jobs: The Great Training Robbery*, Boston: Beacon Press.

BESTOR, ARTHUR (1953) *Educational Wastelands: A Retreat from Learning in Our Public Schools*, Urbana, Ill.: University of Illinois Press.

BILDUNGSBERICHT (1970) *Bildungsbericht '70: Bericht der Bundesregierung zur Bildungspolitik*, Bonn: Bundesministerium für Bildung und Wissenschaft.

BORG, W. R. (1965) 'Ability Grouping in the Public Schools', *Journal of Experimental Education* **34**:2, 1–97.

BOULDING, KENNETH E. (1975) 'The Management of Decline', *Change*, June, 8–9 and 64.

BOURDIEU, PIERRE (1964) *Les Héritiers: Les Étudiants et la Culture*, Paris: Éditions de Minuit.

BOWLES, SAMUEL (1971) 'Cuban Education and the Revolutionary Ideology', *Harvard Educational Review* **41**, 472–500.

BOWLES, SAMUEL (1972) 'Schooling and Inequality from Generation to Generation', *Journal of Political Economy* **80**:3, 219–51.

BOWLES, SAMUEL, and HERBERT GINTIS (1972–3) 'IQ in the U.S. Class Structure', *Social Policy* **3**:4–5, 65–96.

BOWLES, SAMUEL, and HERBERT GINTIS (1976) *Schooling in Capitalist America: Educational Reform and the Contradictions of Economic Life*, London: Routledge and Kegan Paul.

BOWMAN, MARY JEAN (1976) 'Through Education to Earnings? A Review of Formal Education and Adult Earnings, by Ingemar Fägerlind; Education, Occupation, and Earnings, by William H. Sewell and Robert M. Hauser; Higher Education and Earnings, by Paul Taubman and Terence Wales', *Proceedings of the National Academy of Education* **3**, 221–92.

BRITISH YOUTH COUNCIL (1977) *Youth Unemployment: Causes and Cures*, Report of A Working Party, British Youth Council (57 Chalton Street, London NW1 1HU).

BROWN, FRANK B. *et al.* (1973) *The Reform of Secondary Education: A Report to the Public and the Profession* (The National Commission on the Reform of Secondary Education, established by the Kettering Foundation), New York: McGraw-Hill.

BURN, BARBARA B. (ed.) (1977) *International Perspectives on Problems of Higher Education: Access, Systems, Youth and Employment*, New York: International Council for Educational Development.

BURT, CYRIL (1946) *Intelligence and Fertility*, Occasional Papers on Eugenics No. 2, London: Hamilton.

BURT, CYRIL (1966) 'The Genetic Determination of Differences in Intelligence: A Study of Monozygotic Twins Reared Together and Apart', *British Journal of Psychology* **57**, 137–53.

BURT, CYRIL (1972) 'Inheritance of General Intelligence', *American Psychologist* **27**:3, 175–90.

CARNOY, MARTIN (1974) *Education as Cultural Imperialism*, New York: David McKay Co.

CARNOY, MARTIN (1977) *Education and Employment: A Critical Appraisal*, Paris: UNESCO: International Institute for Educational Planning.

CARNOY, MARTIN, and HENRY M. LEVIN (1976) *The Limits of Educational Reform*, New York: David McKay Co.

CATTELL, RAYMOND B. (1937) *The Fight for Our National Intelligence*, London: King.

CAUFIELD-FISCHER, DOROTHY (1942) *Youth and the Future*, Washington, D.C.: American Council on Education.

CHRISTIE, NIELS (1971) *Hvis skolen ikke fantes* (If the School Did Not Exist), Oslo: Universitetsforlaget.

CIPPOLA, C. (1969) *Literacy and Development in the West*, Baltimore: Harmondsworth.

COLEMAN, JAMES S. (1961) *The Adolescent Society: The Social Life of the Teenager and Its Impact on Education*, Glencoe: The Free Press.

COLEMAN, JAMES S. (1968) 'The Concept of Equality of Educational Opportunity', *Harvard Educational Review*, **38**:1, 7–37.

COLEMAN, JAMES S. (1975) 'Methods and Results in the IEA Studies of Effects on School Learning', *Review of Educational Research* **45**:3, 335–86.

COLEMAN, JAMES S. *et al.* (1966) *Equality of Educational Opportunity*, Washington, D.C.: U.S. Department of Health, Education and Welfare, Office of Education.

COLEMAN, JAMES S. *et al.* (1974) *Youth: Transition to Adulthood*, Report of the Panel on Youth of the President's Science Advisory Committee, Chicago: The University of Chicago Press.

COMBER, L. C., and JOHN P. KEEVES (1973) *Science Education in Nineteen Countries: An Empirical Study*, Stockholm: Almqvist and Wiksell; New York: Wiley/Halsted Press.

CONANT, JAMES B. (1959a) *The American High School Today*, New York: McGraw-Hill.

CONANT, JAMES B. (1959b) *The Child, the Parent, and the State*, Cambridge, Mass.: Harvard University Press.

COOMBS, PHILIP H. (1968) *The World Crisis in Education: A Systems Analysis*, London: Oxford University Press.

COUNTS, GEORGES S. (1932) *Dare the School Build A New Social Order?* New York: John Day.

COX, C. B., and A. E. DYSON (eds.) (1969) *Fight for Education: A Black Paper*, London: The Critical Quarterly Society, March.

COX, C. B., and A. E. DYSON (eds.) (1970) *Black Paper Two: The Crisis in Education*, London: The Critical Quarterly Society, October.

CREMIN, LAWRENCE A. (1976) *Public Education*, New York: Basic Books.

DeCECCO, JOHN P., and ARLENE K. RICHARDS (1975) 'Civil War in the High Schools', *Psychology Today*, November, 51–6 and 120.

DOBSON, RICHARD B. (1977) 'Mobility and Stratification in the Soviet Union', *Annual Review of Sociology* **3**, 114–85.

DOBZHANSKY, THEODOSIUS (1973) *Genetic Diversity and Human Equality*, New York: Basic Books.

DORE, RONALD (1976) *The Diploma Disease: Education, Qualification, and Development*, London: Allen and Unwin.

EISENSTADT, SAMUEL N. (1971) *From Generation to Generation*, New York: The Free Press.

EKSTEDT, ESKIL (1976) *Utbildningsexpansion: En studie av den högre utbildningens expansion och ekonomins strukturella omvandling i Sverige under efterkrigstiden* (Educational Expansion: A Study of the Expansion of Higher Education and the Structural Change in the Swedish Economy after the War), Uppsala: Almqvist and Wiksell International.

FARIS, ROBERT E. L. (1961) 'Reflections on the Ability Dimension in Human Society', *American Sociological Review* **26**, 835–43.

FAURE, EDGAR *et al.* (1972) *Learning to Be: The World of Education Today and Tomorrow*, London: Harrap.

FINCH, F. H. (1946) *Enrollment Increases and the Changes in the Mental Level*, Applied Psychology Monographs No. 10, Chicago: University of Chicago Press.

AF FORSELL, CARL (1835) *Anteckningar i anledning af en resa till England i slutet av sommaren 1834* (Notes from a Journey to England at the End of the Summer of 1834), Stockholm: Johan Hörberg.

FRANKEL, CHARLES (1973) 'The New Egalitarianism and the Old', *Commentary* **56**, September, 54–66.

FREEMAN, RICHARD B. (1976) *The Over-educated American*, New York: Academic Press.

FREEMAN, RICHARD, and J. HERBERT HOLLOMON (1975) 'The Declining Value of College Going', *Change*, September, 24–31 and 62.

FRIEDRICH, CARL J. (1963) *Man and His Government: An Empirical Theory of Politics*, New York: McGraw-Hill.

GARTNER, ALAN, COLIN GREER, and FRANK RIESSMAN (1973) *IQ and Social Stratification*, New York: Harper and Row.

GINTIS, HERBERT (1973) 'Toward a Political Economy of Education: A Radical Critique of Ivan Illich's *Deschooling Society*', in Ivan Illich *et al.*, *After Deschooling, What?*, New York: Harper and Row, Perennial Library.

GOODMAN, PAUL (1962) *Compulsory Miseducation*, New York: Random House.

GRUNDIN, HANS U. (1975) *Läs- och skrivförmågans utveckling genom skolåren* (Development of Reading and Writing Skills During School Attendance), Stockholm: Liber Läromedel (Utbildnings-forskning, rapport 20).

HALSEY, A. H. (ed.) (1961) *Ability and Educational Opportunity*, Paris: OECD.

HARNISCHFEGER, ANNEGRET, and DAVID E. WILEY (1975) *Achievement Test Score Decline: Do We Need to Worry?*, Chicago: Cemrel Inc.

HÄRNQVIST, KJELL (1975) 'The International Study of Educational Achievement', in F. Kerlinger (ed.), *Review of Research in Education*, Vol. 3, Itasca, Ill.: Peacock, 85–109.

HAVIGHURST, ROBERT J., and PHILIP H. DREVER (1975) *Youth: The Seventy-Fourth Yearbook of the National Society for the Study of Education*, Chicago: The University of Chicago Press.

HECHINGER, FRED (1976) 'Murder in Academe: The Demise of Education', *Saturday Review*, 20 March, 11–18.

HECHINGER, FRED M., and GRACE HECHINGER (1975) *Growing Up in America*, New York: McGraw-Hill.

HERRNSTEIN, RICHARD J. (1971) 'IQ', *Atlantic Monthly* **228**:3, Sept., 44–64.

HERRNSTEIN, RICHARD J. (1973) *IQ in the Meritocracy*, Boston: Little, Brown and Co.

HEW (1973) *Work in America*, Report of a Special Task Force to the Secretary of Health, Education, and Welfare, Cambridge, Mass.: MIT Press.

HILL, JOHN P., and FRANZ J. MÖNKS (eds.) (1977) *Adolescence and Youth in Prospect*, Guildford, Surrey: IPC Science and Technology Press.

HMSO (1967) *Children and their Primary Schools*, A Report of the Central Advisory Council for Education (England): (Plowden Report) II: Research and Surveys, London: Her Majesty's Stationery Office.

HMSO (1975) *A Language for Life*, A Report of the Committee of Inquiry (The Bullock Report), London: Her Majesty's Stationery Office.

HUSÉN, LENNART et al. (1959) *Elever, lärare, föräldrar: En studie av skolans uppfostrings- och disciplinproblem* (Students, teachers, parents: a study of school discipline), Stockholm: Almqvist and Wiksell.

HUSÉN, TORSTEN (1960) 'Loss of Talent in Selective School Systems', *Comp. Educ. Review* **48**:2, 70–4.

HUSÉN, TORSTEN (1962) *Problems of Differentiation in Swedish Compulsory Schooling*, Stockholm: Svenska Bokförlaget—Scandinavian University Books.

HUSÉN, TORSTEN (1972) *Social Background and Educational Career*, Paris: OECD.

HUSÉN, TORSTEN (1974a) *The Learning Society*, London: Methuen.

HUSÉN, TORSTEN (1974b) *Talent, Equality and Meritocracy*, The Hague: Martinus Nijhoff.

HUSÉN, TORSTEN (1975) *Social Influences on Educational Attainment*, Paris: OECD (Also in French and German).

HUSÉN, TORSTEN (1977a) *Utbildning för jämlikhet? Perspektiv på utbildningsreformerna* (Education for equality? Perspectives on the school reforms), Stockholm: Natur and Kultur.

HUSÉN, TORSTEN (1977b) 'Pupils, Teachers and Schools in Botswana: A National Evaluative Survey of Primary and Secondary Education', in *Education for Kagisano: Report of the National Commission on Education*, Vol. 2, Annexes, Gaborone, Botswana, April.

HUSÉN, TORSTEN (ed.) (1967) *International Study of Achievement in Mathematics: A Comparison of Twelve Countries*, Vol. I–II, Stockholm: Almqvist and Wiksell; New York: Wiley.

HUSÉN, TORSTEN et al. (1969) *Talent, Opportunity and Career: A Twenty-Six-Year Follow-Up of 1,500 Individuals*, Stockholm: Almqvist and Wiksell.

HUSÉN, TORSTEN et al. (1973) *Svensk skola i internationell belysning I: Naturorienterande ämnen* (Swedish Schools in International Perspective, Vol. I: Science), Stockholm: Almqvist and Wiksell International.

HUTCHINS, ROBERT M. (1953) *The Democratic Dilemma*, The Gottesman Lectures, Uppsala University 1951, Stockholm: Almqvist and Wiksell.

IBRD (1976) *World Tables 1976 from the Data Files of the World Bank*, Baltimore and London: The Johns Hopkins University Press.

ILLICH, IVAN (1970) *Deschooling Society*, New York: Harper and Row.

INKELES, ALEX (1974) *Becoming Modern*, Cambridge, Mass.: Harvard University Press.

JENCKS, CHRISTOPHER et al. (1972) *Inequality: A Reassessment of the Effect of Family and Schooling in America*, New York and London: Basic Books.

JENSEN, ARTHUR R. (1969) 'How Much Can We Boost IQ and Scholastic Achievement?', *Harvard Educational Review* **39**, Winter, 1–123.

JOHANSSON, EGIL (1973) *Literacy and Society in a Historical Perspective— A Conference Report*, Umeå: Department of Education, University of Umeå.

JOHANSSON, EGIL (1977) *The History of Literacy in Sweden in Comparison with Some Other Countries*, Umeå: Department of Education, Report No. 12, University of Umeå.

KAMIN, LEON J. (1974) *The Science and Politics of IQ*, Potomac, Md.: Lawrence Erlbaum Associates.

KARABEL, JEROME, and A. H. HALSEY (eds.) (1977) *Power and Ideology in Education*, New York: Oxford University Press.

KATZ, MICHAEL B. (1968) *The Irony of Early School Reform: Educa-*

tional Innovation in Mid-Nineteenth Century Massachusetts, Cambridge, Mass.: Harvard University Press.

KATZ, MICHAEL (1971) *Class, Bureaucracy, and Schools: The Illusion of Educational Change in America*, New York: Praeger Publishers.

KENISTON, KENNETH (1968) *Young Radicals*, New York: Harcourt, Brace and World.

KENISTON, KENNETH (1971) *Youth and Dissent*, New York: Harcourt, Brace and Jovanovich.

KEPPEL, FRANCIS (1966) *The Necessary Revolution in American Education*, New York: Harper and Row.

KERR, CLARK (1977) 'Education and the World of Work; An Analytical Sketch', in James A. Perkins and Barbara Burn (eds.), *International Perspective on Problems in Higher Education*, New York: International Council for Educational Development, 133–42.

LASKA, JOHN A. (1976) *Schooling and Education: Basic Concepts and Problems*, New York: van Nostrand Co.

LAUGLO, JON (1977) 'Educational Change and Aspects of Bureaucratic Organization: The Scandinavian School Reforms', in Ron Glatter (ed.), *Control of the Curriculum: Issues and Trends in Britain and Europe*, London: NFER Publishing House.

LEICHTER, HOPE JENSEN (ed.) (1974) *The Family as Educator*, New York: Teachers College Press, Columbia University.

LESCHINSKY, ACHIM, and PETER MARTIN ROEDER (1976) *Schule im historischen Prozess*, Stuttgart: Klett.

LEVIN, HENRY M. (1972) 'Schooling and Equality: The Social Science Objectivity Gap', *Saturday Review*, 11 November, 49–51.

LEVIN, HENRY M. (1977) *Educational Requirements for Industrial Democracy*, Palo Alto, Calif.: Center for Economic Studies.

LIPSET, SEYMOUR MARTIN (1972) 'Social Mobility and Educational Opportunity', *Public Interest*, No. 29, Fall, 90–108.

LOCKRIDGE, KENNETH A. (1974) *Literacy in Colonial New England: An Enquiry into the Social Context of Literacy in the Early Modern West*, New York: Norton and Co.

LYND, ALBERT (1953) *Quackery in the Public Schools*, Boston: Little, Brown and Co.

MACHLUP, FRITZ (1962) *The Production and Distribution of Knowledge in the United States*, Princeton, N.J.: Princeton University Press.

MACHLUP, FRITZ (1973) 'The Growth of Knowledge Activities in the United States', Presentation at the Autumn Meeting of the U.S. National Academy of Education at Stanford University.

MARKLUND, SIXTEN (1961) *Skolreformen och lärarutbildningen* (School

Reform and Teacher Education), Stockholm: Ministry of Education (1957 års skolberedning).

MARTIN, JOHN H. *et al.* (1974) *Report of the National Panel on High Schools and Adolescent Education*, Washington, D.C.: U.S. Office of Education.

MAXWELL, JAMES (1961) *The Level and Trend of National Intelligence. The Contribution of the Scottish Surveys*, London: University of London Press.

OECD (1962) *Policy Conference on Economic Growth and Investment in Education*, Washington, 16–20 October 1961, Paris: OECD.

OECD (1971a) *Group Disparities in Educational Participation and Achievement*, Background Reports Nos. 4 and 10, Conference on Policies for Educational Growth, Vol. IV, Paris: OECD.

OECD (1971b) *Educational Policies for the 1970s*, General Report, Conference on Policies for Educational Growth, Paris, 3–5 June 1970, Paris: OECD.

OECD (1973) *Recurrent Education: A Strategy for Lifelong Learning*, Paris: OECD.

OECD (1975a) *Education and Working Life in Modern Society*, A Report by the Secretary-General's *ad hoc* Group on the Relations Between Education and Employment, Paris: OECD.

OECD (1975b) *Educational Statistics Yearbook*, Vol. I: *International Tables*, Vol. II: *Country Tables*, Paris: OECD.

OECD (1977a) *Entry of Young People Into Working Life*, General Report, Paris: OECD.

OECD (1977b) *Education Policies. A Report by a Group of Experts*, Paris: OECD.

OECD (1977c) *Selection and Certification in Education and Employment*, Paris: OECD.

OECD (1977d) *Education and Working Life*, Paris: OECD.

ORNSTEIN, ALLAN C., and STEVEN J. MILLER (eds.) (1976) *Policy Issues in Education*, Lexington, Mass.: Lexington Books.

O'TOOLE, JAMES (1977) *Work, Learning, and the American Future*, San Francisco, Calif.: Jossey-Bass.

PASSOW, A. HARRY (1975) 'Once Again: Reforming Secondary Education', *Teachers College Record* **77**:2, 161–87.

PASSOW, A. HARRY, HAROLD J. NOAH, MAX A. ECKSTEIN, and JOHN R. MALLEA (1976) *The National Case Study: An Empirical Comparative Study of Twenty-One Educational Systems*, Stockholm: Almqvist and Wiksell International; New York: Wiley.

PAULSTON, ROLLAND G. (1976) *Folk High Schools in Social Change*, Pittsburgh, Penn.: University Center for International Studies, University of Pittsburgh.

PEAKER, GILBERT F. (1975) *An Empirical Study of Education in Twenty-One Countries: A Technical Report*, Stockholm: Almqvist and Wiksell; New York: Wiley/Halsted Press.

PORTER, JOHN W. *et al.* (1975) *The Adolescents, Other Citizens and Their High Schools: A Report to the Public and Profession* (Task Force '74, A National Task Force for High School Reform, Established by the Kettering Foundation), New York: McGraw-Hill.

POSTLETHWAITE, T. NEVILLE (1967) *School Organization and Student Achievement: A Study Based on Achievement in Mathematics in Twelve Countries*, Stockholm: Almqvist and Wiksell; New York: Wiley.

PUSEY, MICHAEL (1976) *Dynamics of Bureaucracy: A Case Analysis in Education*, New York and Sydney: Wiley.

RAVITCH, DIANE (1977) 'The Revisionists Revised: Studies in the Historiography of American Education', *Proceedings of The National Academy of Education* **4**, 1–84.

RAWLS, JOHN (1971) *A Theory of Justice*, Cambridge, Mass.: Harvard University Press.

REIMER, EVERETT (1971) *School Is Dead*, Middlesex, England: Penguin Books.

RUTKEWITCH, M. N. (ed.) (1969) *The Career Plans of Youth*, White Plains, New York: International Arts and Sciences Press.

RYBA, RAYMOND, and BRIAN HOLMES (eds.) (1973) *Recurrent Education—Concepts and Policies for Lifelong Education*, Proceedings of the Comparative Education Society in Europe Frascati Meeting 1973, London: Comparative Education Society in Europe.

SAUVY, ALFRED, with the co-operation of ALAIN GIRARD, ALBERT JAQUARD, and JANINA LAGNEAU-MARKIEWICZ (1973) *Access to Education: New Possibilities*, Educating Man for the 21st Century, Vol. 4, The Hague: Nijhoff.

SCB (1976) *Högskolestatistik II: Social bakgrund för studerande vid universitet och högskolor 1962/63–1972/73*, Promemorior från SCB 1976:5 (Swedish University Education II: Statistics on Social Background for Students at Universities and Specialized Colleges), Stockholm: Statistiska Centralbyrån, S-10250 Stockholm.

School Review (1974) **82**:1, Special Issue on *Youth—Transition to Adulthood*.

SCHRAG, PETER (1970) 'End of the Impossible Dream', *Saturday Review*, 19 September, 68–69.

SILBERMAN, CHARLES E. (1970) *Crisis in the Classroom: The Remaking of American Education*, New York: Random House.

SOU (1948) *Betänkande med förslag till riktlinjer för det svenska skolväsendets utveckling, avgivet av 1946 års skolkommission* (Report with recommendations about guidelines for the development of the

Swedish school system submitted by the 1946 School Commission), Statens offentliga utredningar, No. 27, Stockholm: Government Printing Office.

SOU (1973) *Högskolan: Betänkande av 1968 års utbildningsutredning* (Higher Education: Report submitted by the 1968 education committee), Statens offentliga utredningar, No. 2, Stockholm: Government Printing Office.

SOU (1974) *Skolans arbetsmiljö. Betänkande avgivet av utredningen om skolans inre arbete—SIA* (The work milieu in the school: Report submitted by the committee on the inner life of the school—SIA), Statens offentliga utredningar, No. 53, Stockholm: Government Printing Office, Ministry of Education.

STATISTISKA CENTRALBYRAN (1976) *Levnadsförhållanden*, Rapport No. 4: Utbildning och studiedeltagande 1974.

SVENSSON, ALLAN (1977) *Jämlikhet och högskoleutbildning. En studie av olika bakgrundfaktorers betydelse för den post-gymnasiala utbildningen* (Equality and Higher Education: A Study of the Significance of Different Background Factors for Post-Secondary Education), Gothenburg: University of Gothenburg, Institute of Education.

SVENSSON, NILS-ERIC (1962) *Ability Grouping and Scholastic Achievement*, Stockholm: Almqvist and Wiksell.

TAUBMAN, P., and T. WALES (1972) *Mental Ability and Higher Educational Attainment in the 20th Century*, A Technical Report Prepared for the Carnegie Commission on Higher Education, Berkeley, Calif.: Carnegie Commission on Higher Education.

TEICHLER, ULRICH (1976) *Das Dilemma der modernen Bildungsgesellschaft*, Stuttgart: Klett.

TEICHLER, ULRICH, DIRK HARTUNG, and REINHARD NUTHMANN (1976) *Hochschulexpansion und Bedarf der Gesellschaft*, Stuttgart: Klett.

THOMSON, GODFREY H. (1950) 'Intelligence and Fertility', *Eugenics Review* **41**:4, 163–70.

THORNDIKE, ROBERT L. (1973) *Reading Comprehension Education in Fifteen Countries: An Empirical Study*, Stockholm: Almqvist and Wiksell; New York: Wiley/Halsted Press.

THUROW, LESTER C. (1972) 'Education and Economic Equality', *Public Interest*, Summer, No. 28, 66–81.

TIMPANE, MICHAEL *et al.* (1976) *Youth Policy in Transition*. Santa Monica, CA: RAND.

TROW, MARTIN (1962) 'The Second Transformation of American Secondary Education', *International Journal of Comparative Sociology* **2**, 144–66.

UNESCO (1974) *Education Statistics Yearbook*, Paris: UNESCO.

UNESCO (1975) *Statistical Yearbook 1974*, Paris: UNESCO Press.

WALKER, DAVID A. (1976) *The IEA Six Subject Survey: An Empirical Study of Education in Twenty-One Countries* (International Studies in Evaluation, Vol. IX), Stockholm: Almqvist and Wiksell International; New York: Wiley.

WATSON, GOODWIN (1945) 'Problems of Bureaucracy', *Journal of Social Issues* **1**, 1–73.

WIRTZ, WILLARD (1975) *The Boundless Resource: A Prospectus for an Education–Work Policy*, Washington, D.C.: The New Republic Book Co.

WRIGHT, A. F., and F. HEADLAM (1976) *Youth Needs and Public Policies*, Melbourne: Department of Youth, Sport, and Recreation, Victoria.

YANKELOVICH, DANIEL (1972) *The Changing Values on Campus: Political and Personal Attitudes on Campus*, New York: Washington Square Press.

YANKELOVICH, DANIEL (1974) *The New Morality: A Profile of American Youth in the 70s*, New York: McGraw-Hill.

YATES, ALFRED (ed.) (1966) *Grouping in Education*, Stockholm: Almqvist and Wiksell.

YOUNG, MICHAEL (1958) *The Rise of the Meritocracy*, London: Penguin.

Index